Send56

Reaching the Unreached of Africa

A Vision for Prayer and Missions

Jesse R. Digges

Printed in the United States of America

First Printing, 2015

ISBN 978-0-9797243-1-2

Gatekeeper Publishing
1625 Collins Hill Road
Lawrenceville, GA 30043

www.Send56.org

Dedicated to my father who introduced me to Christ both in word and deed: a man of grace and compassion, and a faithful minister of the gospel throughout my life. In my youth you encouraged me with 2 Timothy 2:1 to "be strengthened by the grace that is in Christ Jesus." I am still running with that exhortation.

Praise for Send56

I have known Jesse and Rachelle Digges for almost 15 years and have witnessed their deep commitment to Jesus, the prayer movement, and the Great Commission. They are the real deal! Jesse has written a compelling message about bringing the gospel to the unreached of Africa, and given a clarion call for all believers to engage in finishing the Great Commission. The heart behind his pioneering work in East Africa comes through the pages of this book, and it serves as a prototype for the convergence of the prayer and missions movements in the earth today. As you read, I believe that you will be stirred and challenged to give all to Jesus!

Mike Bickle

Director, International House of Prayer Kansas City

Jesse Digges is a dear friend who I am privileged to know. His work in Africa is truly apostolic. The model and vision laid out in this book is a well-rounded prototype for the global church. Those who implement the game plan contained in this book will see the gospel go forward and the gates of hell pushed back in a way that has not been seen since the early days of the Church. I know this because Jesse, the folks at *Send56*, including the African missionaries, have been successfully doing exactly this for some years now. Highly recommended!

Joel Richardson

New York Times Bestselling Author, Preacher, & Film-maker

Candid real life experiential knowledge, speaking challenging truths! OUTSTANDING! A must-read for anyone who desires to further their sold out walk with the Lord. An intense, thought provoking, and educational masterpiece that's full of pertinent information which challenges one to self-inspection, boldness, preparedness, and focus. The build up of real life experiences climaxes with a legitimate call to action. With sound biblical doctrine, Jesse's brilliant expository draws and motivates and challenges in this 'hard to put down' work. Reads like a novel. It empowers all of us to take action today. WELL DONE!

My husband and I have known Jesse and his wife Rachelle, for the past 17 years. We excitedly support and recommend this work.

Patty Cepeda
Author, Business Leader and Life Coach

Right now, prayer and worship are exploding all over the earth, attesting to the worth of Jesus in the nations. It is out of these communities of prayer, worship and ministry to God, that the Lord is raising up dedicated, fearless, skilled and humble missionaries to go to the hardest and darkest places in the earth. Among these missionaries are Jesse and Rachelle, who are pioneering the way for a new generation to give themselves to the Great Commission, specifically in Africa. They are some of our dearest friends, who we have profound respect for. Their zeal for Jesus, their love for Africa, and their tenacious spirit are absolutely astounding. This book will be a manual for the convergence of prayer and missions in the years to come. Get this book.

Corey Russell
International House of Prayer Kansas City

Jesse Digges places a quick and firm hold on our minds and our hearts as he brings fresh light on the global mission of the Church. Detailing the clear opportunity to forge deeper inroads toward unreached people groups, Jesse emphasizes on almost every page the wisdom of incorporating indigenous missionaries into the missions plans of Western churches. Marrying recent trends and current statistics concerning missions and the unreached people groups with his eschatological emphasis on the end of the age, Jesse leads us to address the posture of our hearts toward the end-time harvest. Of particular interest is the emphasis on the rise of Islam and how it impacts the mission of the Church. Establishing some of the clear advantages that native missionaries have, Jesse challenges the reader to consider how much might be accomplished if we support a growing movement of native missionaries. Reading this book will make you want to give all that you can, compel you to go wherever Father might send, and to groan in prayer for those whose feet are already moving in the direction of the unreached people groups on the earth.

Jeff Lyle
Pastor & Founder of Transforming Truth Ministries

Here is a compelling vision of a sovereign God who accomplishes his global purpose, through his people, for his praise among the nations. Here too is a practical invitation to clasp hands across continents, training and sending indigenous workers to reach Africa with the gospel of Christ. Walking with the Digges now for over a decade, I can testify that the vision of *Send56* not only burns in them, but it is also proving effective on the ground. Let this book stir your heart to pray, to give, and to go!

Nathan Tarr
Pastor, Christ Church Knoxville

The books that have impacted me the most have been written by people who are living out what they are calling others to. This is one of those books. I will be giving each of my sons a copy of it with a prayer that they would grow up to live out these principles.

Dalton Thomas
Author, Founder of Frontier Alliance International

What a vision! Jesse Digges, challenges our views of Africa as only a mission field. From the Great Continent there is coming a great sending forth of young fasting and praying firebrands invading the strongholds of Islam. It's happening! Jesse, dream the dream and do it! Read and run with the vision.

Lou Engle
Visionary and Co-founder of The Call

Table of Contents

Forward 3

Acknowledgements 7

Preface 9

1. The Vision 13

2. The Mission and the Challenge 29

3. The Eleventh Hour Workers 61

4. Life Hangs on a Word 81

5. The Testimony of Jesus 115

6. Unceasing Prayer for the Harvest 141

7. Global Partners in the Great Commission 165

Appendix A 191

Appendix B 193

Appendix C 201

Forward

In the Spring of 2012 I was in the middle of a ministry trip to mainland China when the Lord encountered me with truths that would change my life. I had spent the previous week ministering among believers in the world's most populous nation. I was struck by the simplicity of faith and the unmistakable power of the Chinese believers. In the midst of poverty and through great persecution a relatively small remnant of believers had birthed a revival that by some estimates swept over 120 million people into the Kingdom of God. I witnessed first hand the devotion to prayer of the Chinese believers and their dedicated commitment to share the gospel with the lost. Having founded a 24/7 prayer ministry in Atlanta, that has continued without ceasing for over nine years, I generally understood the need for prayer. I am also witness to the growing movement of prayer all around the globe. In China, I began to see how God has ordained that the "prayer movement" with its many global expressions and the missions movement are supposed to be one unified force that would ultimately see the gospel thrust forth to all nations. Prayer and missions were never meant to be separate.

Yet, for whatever reason, prayer and missions are often found to be two independent expressions in the body of Christ. The worship and prayer people on one side, and then the evangelists and missionaries on the other. No longer. The great prayer efforts happening all around the world will inevitably give birth to the greatest missionary advance the world has ever seen. The result will be untold millions of souls swept into the kingdom. This will set the stage for the return of the Lord and His impending reign across the nations.

While in China I was struck by a second revelation. The missions and prayer movement will not be solely or even primarily led by Americans. Instead, God is raising up intercessors and missionaries from many nations that will ultimately carry the flame of the gospel to the hardest and darkest places of the earth. This realization was a blow to my Western pride, but deep in my heart I knew it to be true. If the gospel is going to be preached in every tribe, tongue, people and nation, this will require laborers of multiple ethnicities and backgrounds including Arab, Asian, and African.

The summer of that same year I met Jesse and Rachelle Digges. I had heard of their ministry, but this was the first time I had the opportunity to meet them personally. I was impressed by their focussed vision to raise up prayer centers and missionary schools among African believers and ultimately support and send out native missionaries to the least-reached of Africa. Their vision was in many ways the embodiment of what the Lord had shown me in China - prayer and missions together with a focus on training and sending indigenous workers to unreached people groups.

In the fall of 2014, I had the opportunity to visit the *Send56* base in Uganda. I was encouraged and challenged as I met African missionaries who had been sent to unreached tribes with the gospel. My heart burned as I heard firsthand the stories of unreached people groups hearing and receiving the gospel for the first time through the African missionaries. I was more convinced than ever that God is indeed raising up indigenous workers as a key strategy to see the gospel taken to the ends of the earth.

The book you're holding in your hands will challenge and compel you to labor together with native missionaries. It will cause you to burn with passion for Jesus and a heart for the lost. I encourage you to read prayerfully and allow the Lord to speak to your heart about your role in the burgeoning prayer and missions movement.

Billy Humphrey
Founder & Director
International House of Prayer Atlanta, GA

Acknowledgments

A very special thank you to my amazing wife who encouraged me to write. She put a lot of work into making the book presentable; there is almost nothing I can do without her.

I also want to thank those who helped edit the manuscript. I am indebted to you!

Thank you to Christopher Lyons for the cover artwork.

A special thank you to the International Leader Team for living the values and vision of this book. You are true coworkers in the Lord.

To the faithful laborers I have worked along side in East Africa, the Hodges, the Wambuas, and others.

To the African brethren with whom we work, and who have helped and encouraged this vision over the years, I am grateful for you all.

Finally, to the *Send56* missionaries who are laboring in hard places and laying down your lives for the gospel of Christ: you are the inspiration and truth behind this work.

Preface

Did you know that today there are more Christians living in Africa than there are people who reside in America? Out of this vast harvest is an multitude of men and women whose primary desire is to preach the gospel to the lost. Locations that were once mission fields are now launching pads for sending missionaries who are ready to minister in the most difficult regions of the earth. It is also of great significance that in our day there is a unique opportunity for the Church in the Global North[1] to work together with this missionary force to finish the task of reaching the unreached peoples with the message of Christ.

This book will challenge you to engage in the Great Commission. As I share a little of my own journey as a missionary in Africa, and talk about the role of unceasing prayer, global partnership, and native missionaries, my underlying hope is that you will be inspired to put your own hands to the plow in a global effort to see the gospel reach the ends of the earth. How often we forget the fact that millions are perishing without ever hearing the gospel of Jesus Christ! It is far too rare that believers allow this truth to impact their hearts and shift the way they live their lives.

It is important that I give a brief overview of *Send56* so that you will read with the proper context. What is written has feet to it; and you are invited to run with us! *Send56* is a vision for unceasing prayer and missions to the unreached.

We derive our name from Isaiah 56:7, wherein the Lord declares, "my house shall be called a house of prayer for all peoples." Two powerful truths from this passage guide us like steel tracks guide a train.

First, YHWH, the God of Israel, is the God of all the nations. This is the root and foundation of the Great Commission. The Lord is unquestionably committed to joining a people from every tribe, tongue, and nation, to his house: "Turn to me and be saved, all the ends of the earth! For I am God, and there is no other. By myself I have sworn; from my mouth has gone out in righteousness a word that shall not return: 'To me every knee shall bow, every tongue shall swear allegiance." (Isaiah 45:22–23). God's plan to gather the nations to himself is through the name of Jesus: "so that at the name of Jesus every knee should bow, in heaven and on earth and under the earth, and every tongue confess that Jesus Christ is Lord, to the glory of God the Father" (Philippians 2:10–11).

Secondly, God's house is a house of prayer. Prayer is both the *means* of fulfilling the mission and it is the *end* of it. The Great Commission is about gathering the nations to love and worship God through prayer. We are committed to unceasing prayer in the spirit of the Moravian missions movement of the 18th century, becoming a catalyst for training and sending 10,000 native missionaries to the remaining 1,000 unreached tribes of Africa.

The Lord is raising up native African missionaries who are crucial in bringing the message of Christ to these mostly Islamic regions. We exist as a ministry to serve this movement by creating a bridge for believers in the Global North to join these gospel workers in reaching those without a witness. This is accomplished in the same way John exhorted Gaius to become a "fellow worker" with the traveling missionaries who had stayed with him—by sending them out with support (3 John 5-8). I pray you are motivated and energized as you read this testimony of how God is moving in this generation, and the vital role you have to play.

1. Global North is a term denoting countries (mostly in the northern hemisphere) comprised of North America, Europe, and parts of East Asia. The term is more related to socio-political and economic divide than geography. North America and Europe alone hold more than sixty percent of global wealth. The term Global South conversely speaks of countries mostly in the southern hemisphere (including those in South America, Africa, South and Central Asia) which, generally speaking, hold much less socio-economic and political power. I use these terms interchangeably with "West" and "East" and sometimes "First World" and "Third World" which are outdated and less accurate descriptions of the divide.

1

The Vision

One billion people live in Africa. This vast and diverse continent has been the stage for some of the most dramatic and disturbing events in history, filled with stories of slavery, poverty, genocide, and war.

But I am not writing about the "Dark Continent," as others have called it. I am writing about a radiant one—a place and a people media outlets have largely failed to bring to the world's attention in its proper light. My first visit to Africa was a trip to Uganda in 2007. I had heard the terrible stories about Joseph Kony and Idi Amin, but very little about how God was moving and redeeming the nation. Stories about child soldiers were so infamous and dominant that I half expected to meet Kony at the airport. What I found instead were some of the most joyful and enthusiastic people on the planet, who seemed, in spite of difficult circumstances, to love God in a way that defied every grave report I'd heard.

I will never forget my first time visiting the home of a poor African widow. I noticed a medium-sized turkey, tied by the leg with banana fibers to a short stick frame, set behind two grass-thatched huts made from mud and cow dung. The youngest child, dressed in a tattered shirt and naked from the waist down, was sitting in the dirt staring up at us. This widow lived with four children and two grandchildren. She brought out her only chair, and invited me to sit on it as she knelt in the dirt to greet me in her plain, soiled skirts. She held my hand with rough callused fingers, and smiled up at me, radiant and pleased. I became quite uncomfortable looking into her joyful face. I was not used to kneeling. I couldn't justify this poor woman giving me so much respect, yet I knew that hindering her would be a mistake. Later that day, my heart sunk when her children carried us that strange turkey as a gift. We wouldn't be able to keep it. There was no way to take it on the flight home. And this was their food! This reverse-generosity was incredibly uncomfortable. This widow was loving and honoring us the way most Ugandans would—for her, it was a blessing to receive visitors, and to give even out of her poverty. This kind of giving and hospitable spirit exemplifies the bright nature of many African people.

Before my wife and I moved to Uganda as missionaries in 2008, I went on a short-term mission trip to work for two weeks with a select group of African young adults. Our purpose was discipleship and evangelism. My heart was stirred by the passion these young men and women had for God. As we prayed together daily, the presence of God would rest on our team with tears, prophecy, and cries for revival. I saw their sincere faith and desire for God. We went out to the markets to do evangelism. I witnessed their intense boldness.

No one was shy about Jesus. No one hesitated to proclaim the gospel, in song or in preaching. On one of those crusades, my friend and I prayed for a woman with some type of bulge in her stomach. My African friend, a 19-year-old with rare confidence in God, commanded the growth to be dissolved in Jesus name. Almost immediately, the woman we were praying for was jumping up and down and testifying to the crowd that had spontaneously gathered that she was healed. The swelling in her stomach was gone. As a result, others rushed in to be prayed for and many began to believe the gospel. Today, that young man is a missionary to Muslims in Ethiopia. That trip changed the trajectory of our lives. I became convinced that the youth of Africa will impact the world for Christ.

Africa has a massive destiny in the Kingdom of God. In Africa, there is sin, corruption, and poverty; in America there is sin, corruption, and prosperity. The great difference is that, in their poverty, the African Church has been driven to prayer, from prayer to testimony, and from testimony to praise.

The Church in Africa loves to praise God. African churches often hold all-night prayer meetings. Most who attend these meetings are young people who love to pray, worship, and seek God. Thousands of youth are gathering weekly for all-night prayer all over Africa. One of the first times I attended an "overnight," I was healed of chronic back pain that had been stealing precious sleep for several years.

The African Church has a deeply-rooted prayer culture. Fasting and prayer are regular parts of life for African Christians. Every day of the week in many major towns, you can attend a citywide lunch hour prayer meeting for workers on their lunch break, dedicating that time to the Lord. From prayer mountains to prayer altars, prayer from Africa is filling the bowls of heaven (Revelation 5:8).

In my early twenties, I received a strong personal calling from the Lord to focus my life on bringing the gospel to Muslims. Over the next couple of years, my wife and I prepared to enter the mission field. During this season, two books made a large impression on what would later shape our vision and ministry. The first was Back to Jerusalem, sharing a vision for Chinese missionaries to plant churches along the Silk Road all the way to Israel. The second was Revolution in World Missions, a book about raising up and sending native missionaries from India to go north and reach the unreached Islamic and Hindu people groups of India and greater Asia. We became convinced that native missionaries from the Global South were having great impact in reaching the unreached Islamic world, and that our part, wherever we stationed, would be to serve the native missions movement God was already raising up.

After touching the ground in Uganda, and seeing the zeal, and the sheer number of youth committed to Christ, fireworks started going off in my soul. If there is a Back to Jerusalem movement in China, sending workers along the Silk Road, there needs to be a Back to Jerusalem movement in Africa, sending workers north along the Nile. Not a vision to plant more churches in already well-evangelized areas, but a vision that unites existing churches to train and mobilize African missionaries and send them northward to unreached Islamic people groups where one quarter of the global population of Muslims live. There is a *Gospel for Asia* movement; there should also be a *Gospel for Africa* movement, which empowers African missionaries to reach unreached tribes and communities in the continent. That is when *Send56* began to take shape. Now, after having lived in Africa, laboring for that very vision, I have no doubt that God is using and is going to use in an increasing measure, native African missionaries on the front lines of the Great Commission. It is vital that the Church in the Global North get behind these courageous servants of God.

Africa is viewed by most in the West as a place that needs missionaries—not a place that produces missionaries. Most Westerners think Africans need them, never considering that they need Africans. This superiority complex can lead Western Christians to approach foreign missions with a posture of paternalism resulting in dependency, rather than empowerment. The key to fulfilling the Great Commission is partnership, which assumes equality and interdependence. Fulfilling the Great Commission is a realistic and biblical goal for the Church, and I believe African missionaries will be vital in meeting that goal. We must work together to see the greatest impact.

As I meditate on what God is doing, raising up workers from the poorest countries of the Global South, I am stunned by his goodness and sovereignty. God is showing his grace and power through and among the poorest and most despised of the earth. True impact will not come through the richest in wealth or the best educated, but through the richest in faith. The most overlooked and unrecognized people on the earth, people the world considers powerless, will be beautified with purpose and dignity through their role in God's redemptive plan for humanity. The last shall be first.

Africans Preach a Gospel of Power

Thousands in Africa *live* to preach the gospel. This is the fruit of massive spiritual revivals, which have inspired a generation of believers marked by faith, boldness, and wholehearted belief in the power of God to deliver and heal. The poor economic reality of Africa has not hindered this passion—poverty has actually been the seedbed for its development. Faith is cultivated in the midst of harsh circumstances, where dependence on God for daily provision is a regular event. James says, "Listen, my beloved brothers, has not God chosen those who are poor in the world to be rich in faith and heirs of the kingdom, which he has promised to those who love him?" (James 2:5). Temporal poverty is opportunity for rich and eternal faith. There is simply no way to fill the gap of faith with material things.

The gospel going forth in Africa is not primarily expressed with intellectual prowess, but is an exercise in power and demonstration. There is, of course, great need for the intellect within ministry, but there is also desperate need for demonstration. Witchcraft and idolatrous cultural beliefs have kept people in Africa bound for countless generations, and it is only a gospel demonstrated in power that can bring deliverance to the multitudes.

If you interviewed the average African family, you would find a common theme of regular struggles with spiritual issues related to witchcraft and shamanism. Add to this family feuds, polygamy, rampant sickness, lack of adequate health services, and poverty, and you have a situation primed for the mercy of God. The undeniable power of the gospel addresses these needs directly, and is leading many people to follow Christ.

One Sunday morning, a week after an open-air meeting where our team had prayed for about one hundred new converts, a Muslim man told me that he had given his life to Christ. He had been afflicted by evil spirits, some nights finding himself miles from his home after going to sleep, not knowing how he got there. He was addicted to alcohol and could not get free, spirits also driving him in this addiction. After accepting Christ and receiving prayer, he was completely set free from addiction and spiritual oppression. That is the gospel of power. It addresses the practical needs of a very spiritual culture.

In Muslims, Magic, and the Kingdom of God, Rick Love says that of the world's Muslim population, "conservatively we can conclude that over three-quarters of the Islamic world are folk Muslims," and as many as 95 percent of Muslim women practice an animistic form of Islam.[1] Folk Islam is a form of Islam mixed with spiritism. Love quotes one evangelist to Muslims who called folk Islam "the most pressing issue we face in reaching Muslims."

I have heard this firsthand. A friend and former Muslim told me that at a certain time of the year he used to recite the Qur'an, and he would be taken in a vision to the bottom of a well, where he received special powers and insight from spirits. His salvation story involved deliverance from these very spirits which empowered him under Islam. One day, he heard Jesus call his name and tell him to "get saved" while he was leading prayer in the mosque. He was shaken by the experience, and knew he could not ignore the voice. He went to where some local Christians were having an open-air crusade. He approached them, sweating and in turmoil because of demonic spirits afflicting his mind. Somehow, he knew that he must be saved to be free of them. So he asked the Christian leaders to pray for him. At first, they thought he was lying to them. He was notorious for his opposition to the gospel. Finally, they prayed for him and cast out the demons. He came into a relationship with Christ and his life was changed.

A prominent African evangelist in Uganda and former Muslim explained to me that it is a common belief of Muslims that one can consult jinn (spirits) for help in their personal lives. According to the Qur'an, some of these jinn are actually Muslim spirits who have submitted to Allah after hearing the Qur'an. Bill Musk confirms this in his book, The Unseen Face of Islam. "The fear of jinn, or the desire to subdue and use their services, are strong motivating forces in the practice of ordinary Muslims," Musk says.[2]

Folk Muslims value the meaning of their dreams. They worry about the "evil eye," jinn, and many other things foreign to most Westerners. When we approach this culture with a neat, purely intellectual gospel with no practical ability to overcome these and other issues they are dealing with, we fail to truly impact their everyday reality. David Garrison has written one of the most relevant and needed books in recent times, on understanding how Muslims are coming to Christ, called A Wind in the House of Islam: How God Is Drawing Muslims around the World to Faith in Jesus Christ. His discussion of West Africa could not be more relevant for our topic:

> In both the Muslim north and the Christian south, African Tribal Religion still occupies the beating heart of many ostensibly Muslim and Christian adherents. For many West Africans who are neither Muslim nor Christian, daily life is a struggle with witchcraft and

sorcery. The practical question they face is, "What religion is powerful enough to protect me from the spiritual forces around me?" Western expressions of Christianity which emphasize rational precepts, doctrines and programs have little currency in such an environment, yet when the gospel boldly offers the power to defeat the challenges of curses, physical illness, mental illness, and demonic possession, it is welcomed.[3]

Missiologists have acknowledged the need for the gospel to bring about a power encounter,[4] but what is not discussed very often is how native missionaries (in this context Africans), are so effective in this realm. I want to continue with Musk for a moment, and further illustrate why African missionaries are so well equipped to handle this issue of necessary power encounters:

> Missions is not so much a matter of trying to convey primarily intellectual information, against most of which the Muslim is already inoculated,...It is a question, rather, of preaching the gospel with power, with the Holy Spirit, and with deep conviction as well as with words....Our look at popular Islam pushes the issue of the kingdom of God to the forefront. In so doing, it confronts the Christian evangelist (especially if he is a Westerner) with a dilemma. In their beliefs and practices, ordinary Muslims focus attention on the same issues that brought about so many dynamic encounters in the ministry of Jesus, Paul and others. People are sick and in need of healing: by magic, or by Christ? People require help in a world of hostile,

> occult 'beings': by alliance with evil spirits or with the Holy Spirit? People desire guidance in making important decisions about the future: by fortune-telling and divination, or by Holy Spirit revelation? In popular Islam, there is almost complete allegiance to the kingdom of darkness in the search for such assistance.[5]

Musk addresses this issue, and the dilemma it presents to Westerners in general:

> At the same time, however, the very view of reality that gives rise to the beliefs and practices of ordinary Muslims is in many respects far closer to the biblical one than to the missionary's own mechanistic, scientistic worldview...If the Western believer ever comes to be faced with the details of folk Islamic beliefs and practice, is he able to deal with those phenomena as real entities? Or does he view them as invalid, because his worldview claims that there are no such things as jinn, qurinat, or zodiacal influences? Perhaps he sees the ordinary Muslim as 'primitive'; after all, sickness is explicable simply by germs, not by the evil eye or sorcery. Will his ensuing activity be one of spiritual power encounter or Western education?[6]

It would be hard to find an African missionary with a "mechanistic, scientistic worldview," one who did not believe in spiritual "phenomena as real entities," or one who did not feel and understand the need for God's deliverance from the power of the demonic spiritual world. Most Africans have simply not been influenced by the atheism and secularism of the West, or the Platonic way of thinking in Western Christianity that distinguishes so sharply between the spiritual and physical realms. This means they have little hindrance to belief that spiritual things are real, and that spiritual things affect life in very tangible ways. On the contrary, it may be relevant to warn some believers in Africa against what the apostle Paul calls "irreverent and silly myths" that stem from cultural practices and beliefs, and direct them to a more biblical understanding of the unseen realm (1 Timothy 4:7).

In Garrison's analysis of East Africa, in which there are 298 Muslim people groups, he shows that Muslims are coming to the Lord in great measure because of the power of God:

> Among rural Muslims, Islam is grossly infused with African Tribal Religion; practices of witchcraft, fear of evil spirits, curses, and disease bind the local population to the controls of *Imams* (mosque leaders) whose functions in the community are not much different from the witch doctors who preceded them. In Jesus Christ, these syncretistic Muslims are finding a power that can free them from their previous bondage and dependence on the Imam....Village Muslims who, generations ago, embraced Islam as another means to manipulate the ever-present threat of spirits and demons, are finding in Christ a power greater than the fears that beset them.[7]

The simple truth for most African believers is that Christ has shown himself to be more powerful than the witchcraft they grew up in, and they are therefore ready to follow him and proclaim his name in power. This may be why the Pentecostal and Charismatic segments of Christianity are having such an impact in Africa—because of an emphasis on spiritual renewal, power, and an open confrontation with the demonic realm that is so binding in the lives of many Africans. It is in the context of this confrontation of such powers that a ministry and ambition of bold proclamation develops. This bold proclamation is seen clearly among African missionaries and preachers, and is the pressing need in the Islamic world.

Native Missionaries Are Next Door to the Unreached

One third of all unreached Muslim people groups are located among the 430 million Muslims in Sub-Saharan and North Africa. Close to them, are millions of African evangelical Christians.[8] Though I cover this idea more broadly in the third chapter, I briefly note here that the nearness of native missionaries to the unreached is not just geographical, but involves other major areas of importance including economic, political, educational, and linguistic similarities. This means that people who love Christ and who share a similar culture and economic background are relatively near the unreached. It should be seen as significant that tens of thousands who love to preach the gospel and believe in the power of God are, hypothetically speaking, living next door to hundreds of millions of lost Muslims.

African People Are Regularly Confronted with Islam

Christianity and Islam are in a head-on collision in Africa. Islamic apologists are aggressively challenging Christians with the goal of destroying faith in Christ as the Son of God. This comes in different forms, one of which is open-air debate where da'wah (invitation to Islam) preachers challenge Christian pastors to a contest of Scripture knowledge. Out of these confrontations, there have emerged some very bold and effective witnesses of Christ to Muslims. In the 2010 edition of Operation World, it is noted that "the vast bulk of Africa's unreached are Muslims, many of them practicing an African brand of folk Islam. As demonstrated in West Africa, East Africa and elsewhere, sub-Saharan Africans can be extremely effective at winning Muslims to Jesus and are doing so to greater effect than ever."[9] This is, in part, due to the work of bold African evangelists who have honed their message and confronted the false narrative of the Islamists openly. It is not uncommon to hear testimonies of former Muslims who believed in Christ because they heard courageous preaching from someone who had knowledge of both the Qur'an and the Bible.

In the midst of conflict there is an opportunity, built out of necessity, to train men and woman who have hands-on experience with Muslims, and can effectively reach out to them with the gospel. There are evangelists who have already been successful in winning Muslims to Christ, ready to help this effort. Africa is a promising field for raising up an army of bold witnesses, ready to preach the gospel in the Muslim world. Connecting fibers of training, mobilization, and financial support are desperately needed.

A Vision from the Lord

In 2008, I saw a very vivid picture while praying. I saw a birds-eye view of Africa—like looking at a map from above.

The northern area of the map, west to east, was covered by a dark billowing cloud. I saw what appeared to be arrows of light coming out of East Africa, sent with precision into the darkness. I believe the Lord was showing me native missionaries from Africa who would penetrate the Islamic world with the gospel of Christ. Join me now as we look further at the missions challenge that remains before the Church, and at what God is doing in this bright continent called Africa.

1. Love, Rick. *Muslims, Magic and the Kingdom of God: Church Planting among Folk Muslims*. Pasadena, Calif.: William Carey Library, 2000. 22-23.
2. Musk, Bill A. *The Unseen Face of Islam: Sharing the Gospel with Ordinary Muslims at Street Level*. Rev ed. London: Monarch Books, 2003. 33.
3. Garrison, David. "Chap. 10 The West African Room." In *A Wind in the House of Islam: How God Is Drawing Muslims around the World to Faith in Jesus Christ*. Kindle ed. Monument, CO: WIGTake Resources, 2014.
4. Love, Rick. *Muslims Magic and the Kingdom of God*. 111-112.
5. Musk, Bill A. *The Unseen Face of Islam*. 227.
6. Musk, Bill A. *The Unseen Face of Islam*. 227-228.
7. Garrison, David. "Chap. 5 The East African Room." In *A Wind in the House of Islam: How God Is Drawing Muslims around the World to Faith in Jesus Christ*. Kindle ed. Monument, CO: WIGTake Resources, 2014.
8. Naja, Ben. *Releasing the Workers of the Eleventh Hour: The Global South and the Task Remaining*. Pasadena, Calif.: William Carey Library Publishers, 2007. 28.
9. Mandryk, Jason, and Johnstone, Patrick. *Operation World*. 7th ed. Colorado Springs, CO: Biblica Publishing, 2010. 34.

2

The Mission and the Challenge

The road to Moyale, a Northern Kenya town that borders Ethiopia, is a sand and rock highway that stretches through the Chalbi Desert. Shepherds walk the highway with their rugged cattle and camels traveling to water sources scattered abroad. Once, as we drove along this road, one of these shepherds hailed our van to stop, requesting that we give him water to drink. It was the dry season and months can go by without one drop of rain. We gave him some of our water and began to share the gospel, "the water that springs up into eternal life." When our translator asked him if he knew about the gospel of Jesus Christ, he told us that he had no idea who Jesus was. After a brief time of sharing, he willingly accepted to believe the gospel and we prayed with him through the van window to receive Jesus as savior. There are millions throughout Africa just like this man, comprising approximately 1,000 different unreached ethnic groups, who have never heard of Christ, and they are desperate for living water. Hudson Taylor's plea before two thousand Christian leaders in Scotland in the 19th century, millions of unreached Chinese bearing on his very soul, rings true today:

> It will not do to say that you have no special call to China. With these facts before you, you need rather to ascertain whether you have a special call to stay home. ...If however, it is perfectly clear that duty—not inclination, not pleasure, not business—detains you at home, are you laboring in prayer for these needy ones as you might? Is your influence used to advance the cause of God among them? Are your means as largely employed as they should be in helping forward their salvation?...Oh remember, pray for, labor for the unevangelized millions of China, or will you sin against your own soul![1]

At the time he wrote this, Hudson was just beginning China Inland Mission, and would later give his entire life (three children and his first wife would die on the mission field) to reaching China. Rare are the men who have tapped the raging spring of compassion that stirs the heart of God for lost peoples, but once in a while, they burst on the scene of human history and wake up the Church to the Great Commission.

Was Hudson unbalanced when he pleaded with his audience to labor for the unevangelized millions or "sin against your own soul!"? Or, was he in agreement with the very nature of God's unyielding and demanding sacrificial love? I believe the latter. Truth be told, balance is not the way of Christ, or of his apostles. These were men compelled to sacrificial and selfless living that strikes one at times, as overboard and even foolish. Paul even says, "We are fools for Christ's sake" (1 Corinthians 4:10).

This is how deeply Paul desires the Israelites be saved: "For I could wish that I myself were accursed and cut off from Christ for the sake of my brothers, my kinsmen according to the flesh" and "my heart's desire and prayer to God for them is that they may be saved" (Romans 9:3; 10:1). He tells Timothy, "Therefore I endure everything for the sake of the elect, that they also may obtain the salvation that is in Christ Jesus with eternal glory" (2 Timothy 2:10). When he says he is willing to "endure all things," what he referring to is

> imprisonments, with countless beatings, and often near death. Five times I received at the hands of the Jews the forty lashes less one. Three times I was beaten with rods. Once I was stoned. Three times I was shipwrecked; a night and a day I was adrift at sea; on frequent journeys, in danger from rivers, danger from robbers, danger from my own people, danger from Gentiles, danger in the city, danger in the wilderness, danger at sea, danger from false brothers; in toil and hardship, through many a sleepless night, in hunger and thirst, often without food, in cold and exposure. And, apart from other things, there is the

> daily pressure on me of my anxiety for all the churches. (2 Corinthians 11:23–28)

He writes to the Corinthians, "For we who live are always being given over to death for Jesus' sake, so that the life of Jesus also may be manifested in our mortal flesh. So death is at work in us, but life in you….For the Love of Christ controls us" (2 Corinthians 4:11-12; 5:14). This is the same love that controlled Hudson Taylor.

This kind of risk-taking, all-giving love has its origin in the Son of God. God's approach to loving the world is the gospel. In the gospel, Jesus was balanced, right between two cross beams, reconciling the world to God. The gospel reveals two examples of God's extravagant love for fallen man that we should behold as we talk about the mission challenge.

Galaxies of Love Revealed in the Gospel

We need to direct our gaze to the incarnation (the teaching that the Son of God became a man). God went to the heights of his power and the depths of his compassion to save us. The Son of God previously existed in eternal glory, and then came into the world and lived among fallen human beings. "And now, Father, glorify me in your own presence with *the glory that I had with you before the world existed*" (John 17:5).

When the Father sent his Son into the world, it was more than a king becoming a pauper. It was more than a lion becoming an ant. It was far more than an American leaving Western comforts to live in a difficult impoverished tribe. What is it like to leave glory and come down from heaven? This is exactly how the apostle John tells us we can know the love of God: "*In this the love of God was made manifest* among us, that *God sent his only Son into the world,* that we might live through him" (1 John 4:9). The fact that Jesus left heaven and came into the world is an incomprehensible sacrifice.

But this is not all. The river keeps rushing to new depths! John continues in his epistle with a second way that we know love: "*In this is love,* not that we have loved God but that he loved us and sent his Son *to be the propitiation for our sins*" (1 John 4:10). In chapter 3 of the same letter he said it like this, "By this *we know love,* that *he laid down his life for us*" (1 John 3:16). It is not just the incarnation, but that as a man, Jesus also gave his life to placate the wrath of God's justice deserved by sinners.

These are galaxies of love unfathomable. Jesus said, "Greater love has no one than this, that someone lay down his life for his friends" (John 15:13), and yet Jesus did something "greater" than this. He laid down his life for his enemies!

> For one will scarcely die for a righteous person—though perhaps for a good person [ie. a friend] one would dare even to die—but God shows his love for us in that *while we were still sinners,* Christ died for us....For if *while enemies* we were reconciled to God by the death of his Son, much more, now that we are reconciled, shall we be saved by his life. (Romans 5:7-10)

This is why Paul says to the Ephesian believers that the love of God, "surpasses knowledge" (Ephesians 3:19). It is like looking into the Grand Canyon and trying to determine its breadth with our hand. We don't have the capacity for full comprehension of the depths of God's love. This incarnational, sacrificial love is the fountain of missions that we must draw from if we are to face the challenges before us.

Compassion for the Multitudes

Jesus displayed this love with every day of his life. In Matthew 9:35-38, we get a little snapshot of the ministry that Jesus was carrying out in Israel, and his compassion for the multitudes:

> And Jesus went throughout all the cities and villages, teaching in their synagogues and proclaiming the gospel of the kingdom and healing every disease and every affliction. When he saw the crowds, *he had compassion for them,* because they were *harassed and helpless,* like sheep without a shepherd. Then he said to his disciples, *'the harvest is plentiful,* but the laborers are few; therefore pray earnestly to the Lord of the harvest to send out laborers into his harvest.

As Jesus moved about teaching, preaching, and healing in Galilee and Jerusalem, he was immersed into the needs of the masses. By this time, Jesus' fame was spreading everywhere. Chapter 4 gives a similar snapshot of Jesus' ministry, but shows the condition of the people: "So his fame spread throughout all Syria, and they brought him all the sick, those afflicted with various diseases and pains, those oppressed by demons, epileptics, and paralytics, and he healed them" (Matthew 4:24).

Harassed and *helpless* is a state of hopelessness. It is the state of the multitudes. The primary reason why the multitudes are hopeless is a lack of adequate leadership, "like sheep without a shepherd." The religious aristocracy of Jerusalem had failed to release them from the grip of sin, the binding power of demons, or to deliver them from the crippling weight of sickness, disease, and poverty. Jesus had a scathing indictment for them:

> The scribes and the Pharisees sit on Moses' seat...they preach but do not practice. They tie up heavy burdens, hard to bear, and lay them on people's shoulders, but they themselves are not willing to move them with their finger....
>
> ...For you shut the kingdom of heaven in people's faces. For you neither enter yourselves nor allow those who would enter to go in....
>
> ...For you tithe mint and dill and cumin, and have neglected the weightier matters of the law: justice and mercy and faithfulness. (Matthew 23:2-4, 13, 23)

The people were at the mercy of hypocrites, and it left them in shambles.

Is it so different today? In many parts of the world it is worse! I grieve over the condition of people I see in different parts of the world. In the Somali region of Ethiopia, there is an old walled city which has been dominated by Islam for generations. Dozens of homeless people sleep along the ancient walls that wrap around the city. Mothers raise their babies on the streets. This prompted one of the African missionaries to start a program to provide milk for street babies. There is a small village among another tribe in Northern Kenya where a community of divorced women and widows are outcasts from society. They make up their own community of impoverished single women and moms who have no worth according to the judgment of the society around them.

In Northern Uganda, a tribe called the Karamojong is scorned by much of society as backward and worthless. Many of them have lived a life of violence and fear, being taught from childhood that you are not a man until you have killed. Cows are sacred to the Karamojong, and are their primary source of livelihood. For many years, cattle raiding has been commonplace. I remember talking with a poor woman, in a grass-thatched hut with no walls, who later gave her life to Christ. She described to me that her husband had been killed three weeks before we arrived by cattle raiders. How is this widow to take care of herself and her children when she is left with nothing? Millions across Africa and across the world are like this, *harassed* and *helpless,* and for many there is simply no hope of getting out of poverty, sickness, and oppression. Government and religious leaders are often guilty, not of relieving the burden, but of heaping on top of it with corruption and injustice.

The text states that Jesus "saw the crowds," and "he had compassion for them." I have a theory that when he saw the crowds, he was not just seeing his immediate audience, but the billions of his elect throughout time and generations. This word "crowds" is used in Revelation 7:9; 17:15; 19:6 to refer to the "multitudes" of the nations. When you consider Jesus' next statement that the "harvest is plentiful," it seems that we cannot confine the multitudes he is seeing to the immediate crowd in front of him. I believe this immediate crowd reminded Jesus of the global harvest in all the nations that are "harassed," "helpless," and without a shepherd. Jesus is seeing billions of lost souls his Father sent him to die for, not just the thousands in Jerusalem before him in that moment.

This does not lessen the extent of compassion that he had for the Israelites, it only broadens and intensifies it.

In Matthew 23, after scolding the religious leadership of Israel and showing them how they had turned away from God, he reveals his heart of love for them: "O Jerusalem, Jerusalem, the city that kills the prophets and stones those who are sent to it! How often would I have gathered your children together as a hen gathers her brood under her wings, and you would not! Therefore your house is left to you desolate" (Matthew 23:37-38).

The consequence of not embracing Jesus as their Messiah and King is being left in desolation. But how he longs to gather them! And to care for them! How he has compassion for them. So he goes on to declare their judgment and their hope. A day is coming when they will embrace his leadership, but not now, "For I tell you, you will not see me again, until you say, 'Blessed is he who comes in the name of the Lord'"(Matthew 23:3).

I will let Paul summarize what is happening here: "Lest you be wise in your own sight, I do not want you to be unaware of this mystery, brothers: a partial hardening has come upon Israel, until the fullness of the Gentiles has come in. And in this way all Israel will be saved, as it is written, 'The Deliverer will come from Zion, he will banish ungodliness from Jacob'" (Romans 11:25–26).

The destiny of Israel is that they will be saved. The deliverer will come out of Zion, but first they are hardened until the fullness of the Gentiles comes in. After that time, the Jews will be provoked to jealousy, and finally invite Jesus to reign over Israel. This will mark the beginning of the end of satanic influence in the world, and Jesus the good Shepherd will lead the earth into prosperity from Jerusalem. This is what David sang about in Psalm 22:26-28: "The afflicted shall eat and be satisfied; those who seek him shall praise the LORD! May your hearts live forever! All the ends of the earth shall remember and turn to the LORD, and all the families of the nations shall worship before you. For *kingship belongs to the LORD*, and he rules over the nations." Paul says it like this in Romans, quoting Isaiah the prophet: "The root of Jesse will come, even he who arises to rule the Gentiles; in him will the Gentiles hope" (Romans 15:12/Isaiah 10:11).

My final note on Matthew 9:35-38 involves what Jesus' compassion moved him to say: "The harvest is plentiful, but the laborers are few; therefore pray earnestly to the Lord of the harvest to send out laborers into his harvest." God's solution to the enormity of the harvest is to send laborers. Laborers are disciples of Christ who are in agreement with his heart of compassion for the harassed and helpless, and who are willing to be sent in order to introduce them to another kingdom, in which they will find their deliverer. The problem is not the vastness of the harvest. That is a good thing! The problem is that there are not enough people like Paul the apostle or like Hudson Taylor who are in agreement with Jesus' compassion for the harvest; the compassion that moved Jesus to leave heaven and die for the salvation of the nations. The passion that made him give all.

In John 4:35-36, Jesus invites his disciples to see the harvest and participate in that compassion: "Do you not say, 'there are yet four months, then comes the harvest'? Look, I tell you, *lift up your eyes, and see that the fields are white for harvest*. Already the one who reaps is receiving wages and gathering fruit for eternal life, so that the sower and reaper may rejoice together."

The disciples were not seeing what Jesus was seeing. Just before this, they are perplexed by his conversation with a Samaritan woman, who was an outcast (to the Jews), and a sinner. They saw someone who was not worth his time. Jesus saw the harvest. They felt hunger. Jesus felt compassion. Jesus' compassion for this woman and his commitment to the will of the Father led him to live a very unbalanced life. Sometimes he would even forget to eat: "Meanwhile the disciples were urging him, saying, 'Rabbi, eat.'... Jesus said to them, 'My food is to do the will of him who sent me and to accomplish his work'" (John 4:31-34).

Many people are so distracted with trivial pursuits that they do not perceive the heart of God for the harvest. They do not see it. They see only the things, whether obligations or desires, right in front of them. Many are suffering from *mall syndrome*. People in the mall are called consumers not just because they consume but because they are being consumed. The latest technology, clothes, movies, food, are all vying for the attention of the mind and heart. In many ways, this is a parable for much of Western Christianity. Our eyes are locked on so much *stuff* that we become blind to the desires of God. Jesus gives a challenge and an invitation; he says, "lift up your eyes!" and see as he sees. Today's great need is for people who are consumed not with consuming, but with the compassionate heart of the Lord of the harvest.

What Is the Mission?

The harvest is personal for Jesus because it is his harvest. He has an inheritance from the Father among all the nations and tribes of the earth, and he *must* have them. "The Lord said to me, 'You are my Son; today I have begotten you. Ask of Me, and I will make the nations your heritage, and the ends of the earth your possession'" (Psalm 2:7-8). Ephesians 1:18 shows this also, when Paul prays for the Church in Ephesus: "that you may know...what are the riches of his glorious inheritance in the Saints." The saints are the Son's inheritance. When Jesus prays for the Church in John 17, he literally fulfills the command of the Father in Psalm 2. He asks his Father to give him all believers throughout the ages: "I do not ask for these only, but also for those who will believe in me through their word,...Father I desire that they also, whom you have given me, may be with me where I am" (John 17:20; 24). The desire of the Son is that his great global inheritance, believers from all ethnic groups of the earth, would be with him, beholding and enjoying his glory, forever.

Psalm 2 is talking about more than just individual people. It refers to nations. Not nation states like we have today, but tribes or ethnic groups like the Berber in Sudan, or the Garreh of Kenya, or the Somalis in the Horn of Africa. The Great Commission is not just preaching to as many *people* as possible, but bringing a witness to as many *peoples* as possible. In John Piper's crucial work, Let the Nations be Glad! The Supremacy of God in Missions, he shows how Matthew 28:18-20, the primary Great Commission passage in the New Testament, is about people groups and not just Gentile individuals:

> God's call for missions in scripture cannot be defined in terms of crossing cultures to maximize the total number of individuals being saved. Rather, God's will for missions is that every people group be reached with the testimony of Christ and that a people be called out for his name from all nations.[2]

The prophetic vision in the book of Revelation is explicit in its broad description of those numbered among the elect[3]: "And they sang a new song, saying, "worthy are you to take the scroll and to open its seals, for you were slain, and by your blood you ransomed people for God, from every *tribe* and *language*, and *people*, and *nation*" (Revelation 5:9).

This distinction of people groups is critical to understand because it gives us the important task of reaching tribes and peoples that are unreached. We are not just called to evangelism in nations where there is already Christian presence, but also to reach places where there is no access to the gospel. The unreached as defined by Joshua Project[4] are people groups where ninety eight percent of the population have no gospel witness. The Church in these places has not become strong enough to self-propagate, and many among them have never even heard of Christ. These are often the most resistant areas to the gospel as we will see below. So what would compel us to reach them? Why not just preach in places that are responsive? What makes us go beyond Jerusalem, Judea and Samaria, to the ends of the earth? The answer is found in a biblical definition of what the mission of the Church is, which will be discussed more fully in the 4th chapter.

Why the Unreached Are Unreached

Simply put, the unreached are unreached because it is hard to reach them. Let's observe some of the primary barriers that are faced when trying to plant churches in these difficult people groups.

Geographic Barriers

Many unreached people groups live in remote places with harsh climates. These areas are often hard to access because of a lack of infrastructure. This is true of some of the Nilotic people groups in East Africa. There is no running water or electricity. In order to share the gospel with the more remote people living in parishes and villages, you have to find your way along foot paths and through a wilderness of thorns and bush. It takes great effort just to reach their Manyatas (stick-framed family compounds) where you can begin to share the gospel. Manyatas are surrounded by a fence made of protruding sticks woven together with thorn bushes, and are inhabited by a clan. Each individual family of the clan has their own space within, usually consisting of a hut with a cow skin on the floor used as a mattress. Each individual space is also barred by a wall of sticks and thorns. The only entrance stands no more than two and a half feet from the ground, which requires the one entering to kneel down and compact their body to get through. The floor of the hut is dug out about two feet beneath the earth to hide the person sleeping from stray bullets.

Choosing to live near these dwellings takes another level of grace entirely. There are no malls, no paved roads, no conveniences, extreme poverty, and unending heat! The people are semi-nomadic and live on a very lean diet only taking one meal a day. Sadly, there is also rampant drunkenness, and most are addicted to a local alcohol made from sorghum flower. You may even find little children drunk from eating the sorghum sediment left over from the drink. It is hard to reach them because it is hard to get to them, and even harder to live with them. But they are the inheritance of Jesus and he *must* have them. In the last couple of decades, the gospel has been bearing great fruit among some of these tribes, the Karamojong and the Maasai in particular. But there is still more to be done, especially among their less reached neighbors, the Teuso, Taposa, Turkana, Reshiat, and other tribes like them scattered across the African continent.

Linguistic Barriers

Illiteracy, unwritten languages, and lack of Scripture in the native language of a specific tribe are some more obstacles to reaching the unreached. One of the greatest ways for the gospel to take root in a given cultural group is for it to be shared in the native tongue of that group, and not just in a trade language. When the gospel takes root in the native language of the people, it has the most potential for impact. We will see later how native missionaries, even uneducated ones, are often well-equipped to overcome some of these linguistic challenges.

Cultural Barriers

Persecution usually happens among peoples who are resistant to change or new ideas. Christianity can be viewed as foreign and dangerous, subverting cultural norms and traditions. For native missionaries, cultural barriers may not be as difficult to overcome, especially if they are from a similar cultural background as the tribe they are reaching. More will be said on this in chapter 3.

The Islamic Barrier

One of the greatest cultural hindrances to the gospel that the world has ever known is the Islamic religion. This is a cultural barrier, because Islam itself creates a culture of intolerance and resistance to the Christian faith. It is easy to imagine what might happen in a person's subconscious, when they grow up learning that Christians are *Kafir* (blasphemers) and unclean. What would you feel about Christians if, from childhood, you knew that they are guilty of the worst kind of sin called *Shirk* (which is to ascribe partners with God), because they say that Jesus is the Son of God. How might you feel about Christians when you became an adult, if as a child you read verses like these:

> They say: '(Allah) Most Gracious has begotten a son!' Indeed ye have put forth a thing most monstrous! At it the skies are ready to burst, the earth to split asunder, and the mountains to fall down in utter ruin, that they should invoke a son for (Allah) Most Gracious (Qur'an 19:88-92)[5]

> The Jews call Uzair a son of Allah, and the Christians call Christ the son of Allah. That is a saying from their mouth; (in this) they but imitate what the unbelievers of old used to say. Allah's curse be on them: how they are deluded away from the Truth! (Qur'an 9:29-31)

Naturally, you might become anti-Christian, and you would resist with force the spread of the gospel of God's Son. That is what Islam is (anti-Christian) and that is what Islam does (resist the gospel). In his book, Church Planting Movements, David Garrison says, "Islamic Sharia constitutes the only major religious system in the world designed to defeat Christianity."[6] This is because resistance to the Christian faith was built into the fabric of the Qur'an, which Muslims hold to be a divine book directly copied from its eternal source in heaven. It is Allah's eternal word. Interestingly, according to Islamic history, many of the ayahs (verses) that refute New Testament doctrines were revealed to Muhammad in Medina when his prophethood was being challenged by Jews and Christians. The polemical bent of the Qur'an against the core doctrines of the Christian faith is undeniable.

The Qur'an doesn't just deny the Sonship of Jesus, it also denies the fatherhood of God. It is remarkable that the apostle John showed the Church how to identify the doctrine of the antichrist: "This is the antichrist, he who denies the Father and the Son" (1 John 2:22). This duel denial defines the spirit of Islamic theology: "(Both) the Jews and the Christians say: 'We are sons of Allah, and his beloved.' Say: 'Why then doth He punish you for your sins? Nay, ye are but men—of the men he hath created'" (Qur'an 5:18). And, "Not one of the beings in the heavens and the earth but must come to (Allah) Most Gracious as a servant" (Qur'an 19:93).

But there is more to be concerned about, for Islam in not just a perversion of theology, but also of soteriology (the study of religious doctrines of salvation). The death of Jesus on the cross is said to be an illusion that did not actually occur, and thus the resurrection of Jesus would also be a hoax. One is stunned by the supposed denial of the crucifixion in the Qur'an, which was separate from the events of the crucifixion by six hundred years and seven hundred miles. It flies against the eyewitness accounts of the New Testament authors and also extra-biblical historical source evidence from Jewish historian Josephus and Roman historian Tacitus, both confirming the crucifixion of Jesus in the late first century and early second. The evidence for the crucifixion is so strong that it has led even leading liberal and critical scholars, like

Dominic Crosson, to say, "That he was crucified is as sure as anything historical can ever be."[7] But here is what the Qur'an says:

> That they said (in boast), 'We killed Christ Jesus the son of Mary, the Messenger of Allah'; but they killed him not, *nor crucified him*, but so it was made to appear to them, and those who differ therein are full of doubts, with no (certain) knowledge, but only conjecture to follow, for of a surety *they killed him not*. Nay, Allah raised him up unto Himself; and Allah is Exalted in Power, Wise. (Qur'an 4:157-158)

This verse does not even specifically deny that the Romans killed Jesus, but Muslims for centuries have been taught that it does. This leads to a complete opposition to the apostolic message of atonement and salvation by grace through faith. The gospel says that we are *not* saved by our own works, so that no one may boast in himself, but through the sovereign and free grace of God. Salvation is accomplished by God for us, through the atoning, justifying work of Jesus on the cross. The righteousness of Christ is imputed to all who believe. Contrary to this, Islam teaches pure legalism, and makes works the means of salvation: "Then those whose balance (of good deeds) is heavy, they will attain salvation. But those whose balance is light, will be those who have lost their souls; In Hell will they abide. The Fire will burn their faces, and they will therein grin, with their lips displaced" (Qur'an 23:102-104).

It is important that we don't gloss over this point. One of Paul's primary struggles in missions was dealing with those who tried to add circumcision and the Mosaic Law as requirements preceding salvation. Romans 10:2-4 is very important for us to understand. In context, it is about Jews, but it is just as pertinent when dealing with Muslim thought: "For I bear them witness that they have a zeal for God, but not according to knowledge. For being ignorant of the righteousness of God, and seeking to establish their own, they did not submit to God's righteousness. For Christ is the end of the law for righteousness to everyone who believes" (Romans 10:2-4).

Muslims are zealous for Allah, but they are "ignorant of the righteousness of God" which Paul says in chapter 1 is revealed through the gospel: "For I am not ashamed of the gospel,...For in it the righteousness of God is revealed from faith to faith, as it is written, 'The righteous shall live by faith'" (Romans 1:16-17). Just as the Jews sought to establish their own righteousness through the Law of Moses, Muslims seek to establish their own righteousness by strict adherence to Sharia (Islamic Law). By fulfilling Islamic Sharia, they prove themselves to be Muslims (one who is submitted to God), and obtain their place in *Jannah* (paradise).

Scripture teaches that we cannot obtain righteousness through the Law but only by receiving the free gift of God's righteousness, which is imputed to believers on the bases of faith in the work of Christ. Seeking to establish their own righteousness apart from Christ, Muslims are actually not submitted to God, but completely disobedient to his primary command, which is to receive a free gift of justification through faith. The irony here is astounding. The message of salvation through faith is what apostolic ministry to the nations is all about: "Through whom we have received grace and apostleship *to bring about the obedience of faith* for the sake of his name among all the nations" (Romans 1:5). If we pit

Islam up to this standard, we quickly see that Islam is anti-gospel.

A rural Islamic community that has never had a gospel witness does not know the good news about Jesus Christ. The Christ they believe in, *Isa al-Masih,* is simply not the same as the Jesus of the New Testament. Therefore, unreached Muslims do not know the Jesus of the Scriptures. They believe he was a Muslim prophet, and though uniquely born to the virgin Mary, sent only to Israel and subservient to Muhammad. Unreached Muslims do not know that Jesus is the Lord, nor have they heard that he is the Son of God who came into the world, died on the cross for sins, and rose again the third day. They do not know the love of our Father God.

From the state to the nuclear family, Islam has proven to be the most aggressive force in hindering Christianity, with an unmatched record of persecution and suppression of the Christian faith. From the death sentence for apostates to imprisonment for anyone who is seen as propagating another faith, Islam has proven to be an oppressive system. On the family level, Islamic cultures are *honor cultures,* and consider shame to be among the worst type of grievance. When a son our daughter leaves Islam to embrace Jesus, the family is often complicit in rejecting or (in the worst cases) killing that family member to remove the disgrace from the family. This is called an *honor killing*. In a less extreme circumstance, the Christian convert is ostracized and denied the ability to work or share in the life of his community, often having to flee to another city or province. Moderate Muslims (there are peaceful Muslims) in America and Europe would like to convince us that Islam is a peaceful religion, but the facts show the opposite. One only has to visit barnabasfund.org and view the world map compiling cases of persecution around the world to observe that Islam ignites much of the world to subjugate and persecute Christians.[8]

Persecution was something that I knew was happening in the Muslim world, but the reality hit home when a friend and associate of ours named Umar Mulinde was attacked in his church parking lot on Christmas Eve, 2011. Umar is a husband and father of six. He grew up as a Muslim, until he heard the gospel preached by someone who knew the Qur'an and the Bible. He was convinced of the truth of the gospel after he had a series of dreams about his eternal destiny. I don't think I have ever known someone who operated with such faith and boldness in evangelism to Muslims. He was never shy of exposing falsehoods in the Qur'an and calling Muslims to come to Jesus, and many did.

I was with Umar just two days before the attack. He was conducting a five-day evangelistic outreach Christmas week, and many people were coming to Christ. The outreach was relatively peaceful, but people were coming to know the Lord, including Muslims. It was Saturday night, the event was ending, and they were setting up the church to receive the new believers who accepted Christ during the open-air meeting. Two men were waiting for Umar in the dark as he made his way from the church to his car. They called for him to come over to them, but he ignored them until they ran up with buckets of acid and shouted "Allahu Akbar!" as they threw it at him. The acid hit one side of his face, but he was left with enough consciousness to dive onto the ground and pull his jacket over his head. The men proceeded to empty the rest of the acid onto his jacket and then fled. In the wake of the attack, the doctors had to remove one of his eyes. He will be permanently scarred on the entire right side of his face and head.

Umar has paid a price for his service to Christ among Muslims. He bears the marks of Christ on his body. The miracle that came out of this is another story, which continues to unfold. He was brought to Israel and treated for free by Israeli doctors, and has had many opportunities to share about his conversion with Jews and Muslims in Israel. He has no plans for silence, and he continues to preach boldly in Uganda.

The Believer's Response to Islam's Challenge

Lets look again in Romans and see how Paul might have instructed believers to respond to Islam: "As regards to the gospel, they are enemies of God for your sake. But as regards election, they are beloved for the sake of their forefathers." For Paul, enemies of the gospel were considered beloved of God. We can hear the teaching of Jesus resounding here: "But I say to you, love your enemies and pray for those who persecute you, so that you may be sons of your father in heaven" (Matthew 5:44-45).

When you love your enemies, you become like God the Father. This brings us full circle. God's love was set upon his enemies, therefore he came and endured the cross. It does no good to say that we don't have any enemies, like some who try to synchronize Christianity with Islam. Islam is an enemy of the gospel, and so are many Muslims. But what are Christians to do with their enemies? The answer is in one word; love. God commands that we love them, this requires that we pray for them, and work for their salvation.

Raymond Lull: Missionary to Muslims

Raymond Lull, considered the first missionary to Muslims, was called the "Fool of Love." He was fifty-six when he initially traveled to North Africa to preach the gospel. He did this in a very politically charged time when most Europeans could only think of fighting Islam militarily. Instead, Lull "planned to attack with the new weapons of love and learning instead of the Crusaders' weapons of fanaticism and the sword."[9] He tried convincing others of the same method. George Smith writes of Lull, "In an age of violence and faithlessness, he was the apostle of heavenly love." Zwemer adds "Raymund Lull believed and proved that love could conquer it (Islam)....His one weapon was the argument of God's love in Christ."

The depth of Lull's devotion to Christ is stunning. He was a man whose whole desire was to live and die for the name of Jesus. He was a self-taught intellectual giant who wrote works in science and philosophy as well as theology, but his main ambition was a mission to the Muslim world. He took nine years to learn Arabic in his forties, and developed the first systematic apologetic to address Islam. He spent countless hours traveling and promoting the cause of Christ among Muslims, to Popes and Kings, requesting participation in founding schools that could train monks in their language and geography. He laments here the difficulty of his task:

> I find scarcely anyone, Oh Lord, who out of love to Thee is ready to suffer martyrdom as Thou has suffered for us. It appears to me agreeable to reason, if an ordinance to that effect could be obtained, that the monks should learn various languages, that they

> might be able to go out and surrender their lives in love to Thee....Oh Lord of Glory, if that blessed day should ever be in which I might see thy holy monks so influenced by zeal to glorify Thee so as to go to foreign lands in order to testify to Thy holy ministry, of Thy blessed incarnation, and of Thy bitter sufferings, that would be a glorious day, a day in which that glow of devotion would return with which the holy Apostles met death for their Lord Jesus Christ.

In spite of this lament, Lull did manage to found a monastery in Majorca training Monks for missionary work among Muslims. Later, he would also succeed in convincing a church counsel in France of his cause. A decree was given that chairs in oriental languages be set up in the important universities of Europe, in order to prepare students to face the Muslim challenge. In this way "he anticipated Loyola, Zinzendorf, and Duff in linking schools to missions; and his fire of passion for this object equaled, if not surpassed their zeal."

At fifty-six, Lull took his first journey to North Africa and traveled by sea to Tunisia. He went alone, into the lion's den. He was not one to secretly preach. He went right for the leaders and challenged them to a dialogue where he could set forth the truths of Christianity. After gaining a hearing and debating his case, he was immediately labeled a dangerous heretic, cast into a dungeon, and banished from the land. Having won some converts, he could not allow them to cast him out, so he escaped his deportation. He then labored for a few more months with a small number of converts before returning to Majorca.

Lull's next missionary journey was to Algeria, now in his early seventies. Of this Zwemer writes, "Raymund Lull no sooner came to Bugia than he found his way to a public place, stood up boldly and proclaimed in the Arabic language that Christianity was the only true faith, and expressed his willingness to prove this to the satisfaction of all." The crowd rose up to do him violence, but the Mufti stopped them and gave time for Lull to plead insanity. His reply? "Death…has no terrors whatever for a sincere servant of Christ who is laboring to bring souls to a knowledge of the truth." Lull was kept for several months in a dungeon, and then sent home a second time.

Some who read this story may feel the same way as the Mufti; this person was insane. I would suggest that if Lull was insane, so was the apostle Paul. He made it a point everywhere he went to visit the synagogue and proclaim openly the gospel of Christ to the Jews. And so was Peter, who decided to preach in Jerusalem just days after they had crucified Christ in the very same city. How many times was Paul lashed with whips, cast out, and left for dead? Yet he continued open proclamation and debate to further the gospel. Lull was not insane; he was in the vein of the apostles. On the other hand, we may observe that he could have been more effective, had he not immediately gotten himself deported. He could have been more careful in order to maintain a longer presence in the country. Had he labored more patiently to win disciples on a person-to-person level before outing himself, his missions may have born more long-term fruit. But even this is human wisdom and speculation. Lull's insane boldness may have broken open the door for future generations of laborers to overcome fear and to lift their voices for the gospel among Muslims.

In his old age, Lull returned to Algeria to testify of Christ to Muslims. This time, it would be the witness of his very life. We rely on Zwemer for the account, and it seems this time he followed a more cautious approach: "For over ten months, the aged missionary dwelt in hiding, talking and praying with his converts and trying to influence those who were not yet persuaded." Finally, the burden of the Lord and love for the lost became too great:

> Weary of seclusion, and longing for martyrdom, he came forth into the open market and presented himself to the people as the same man whom they had once expelled from their town....He pleaded with love, but spoke plainly the whole truth....Filled with fanatic fury at his boldness, and unable to reply to his arguments, the populace seized him, and dragged him out of the town; there by the command, or at least the connivance, of the king, he was stoned on the 30th of June 1315.

That day, Lull wore the crown of witness and joined those under the altar of God, "the souls of those who had been slain for the word of God and for the witness they had borne" (Revelation 6:9).

Such a witness is what conquers the enemy and breaks open the nations to the gospel. But it would be unfair to the reader not to mention the timidity that first accompanied such a warrior for Christ. When he was about to set sail for the first journey to Tunis, Lull was trembling with fear and then overcome. He made the crew remove his books and luggage from the boat and watched it sail away without him. As soon as it was gone, he became ill with remorse at his lack of boldness and faith. This is an encouragement. Lull was a man like any other man, prone to fear and unbelief, in need of the grace of God to fulfill his calling. It is not momentary lapses or failures that prove or disprove courage. I believe, as with Peter, Christ was interceding that Lull's faith might not fail. Soon, he learned of another ship going to the same city, and begged the crew to let him aboard, which they did, and "From this moment he was a new man. The vessel had hardly lost sight of land before all fever left him; his conscience no more rebuked him for cowardice, peace of mind returned, and he seemed to have regained perfect health."

Lull is an inspiration to a generation no less called to missions among Muslims. There is a desperate need for witnesses with faith, boldness, dedication, perseverance, and love. There continues to be a great need to fulfill Lull's vision for missions schools that will raise up faithful witnesses to the Muslim world, teach their language, geography, and then equip these men and women with the apologetics necessary for the Islamic challenge. Today, Islam is more prominent than it was in the thirteenth century, and missionaries among them are no less needed. Both then and now, the peoples that make up the Muslim world are vastly unreached and ignorant of the true gospel. The lost of the Islamic world need an urgent rescue mission of thousands of new workers who are ready to lay down their lives for the sake of Christ. We need to hear the charge Paul gave Timothy:

> And the Lord's servant must not be quarrelsome but kind to everyone, able to teach, patiently *enduring evil, correcting his opponents* with gentleness. God may perhaps grant them repentance leading to a knowledge of the truth, and *they may come to their*

senses and *escape from the snare of the devil,* after being captured by him to so do his will. (2 Timothy 2:24-26)

Multitudes are in a snare, captured by the enemy, held in bondage to his agenda and will. An urgent rescue operation must take place in the Muslim world.

Islam in Africa

According to a recent Pew Research Center analysis of the global population of Muslims, the Islamic population in the world is 1.6 billion.[10] That means that 1 out of 4 people on the planet believe in the Allah of Islam. One quarter of these Muslims are located in Africa. Sub-Saharan Africa has about 241,000,000 Muslims, which is roughly 15% of the world Muslim population. North Africa contains another 190,000,000.[11] Almost half of the billion people that constitute Africa are Muslim. Muslims are the largest demographic with the most unreached people in the world, and only 10% of Christian workers are among them.[12] As I stated in the beginning of this chapter, of the approximately two thousand ethnolinguistic people groups in Africa, one thousand are considered unreached; most of these are Islamic people groups.

Embracing Apostolic Ambition

The question before us is, will we lay hold of Jesus' command and embrace his heart for the nations? Will we receive and agree with his compassion for the nations when he says, "I have other sheep that are not of this fold. *I must bring them* also....My Father who has given them to me, is greater than all" (John 10:16; 29). Jesus *must* bring in all the nations! He will not forget them. Will we make the *must* of Jesus, the ambition of our life?

Paul did. In Romans 15, he says that he made it his singular focus to bring the message of Christ to unreached peoples: "Thus *I make it my ambition* to preach the gospel, not where Christ has already been named, lest I build on someone else's foundation, but as it is written, 'Those who have never been told of him will see, and those who have never heard will understand'" (Romans 15:20-21).

Paul radically oriented his life and ministry toward bringing the gospel to new lands and new peoples who had never heard: "We do not boast beyond limit in the labors of others. But our hope is that as your faith increases, our area of influence may be greatly enlarged, *so that we may preach the gospel in lands beyond you*" (1 Corinthians 10:15-16). He knows that as the faith of the Corinthians expands and more people respond to the gospel, new doors will be opened among the unreached. The unreached were his end game.

What would it look like if the unreached became the aim of life? How would it change major decisions or directions one might pursue? Like the purpose for going to college or the reason for business or ministry? What a person thinks of when they go to bed and when they wake up is good indication of their ambitions. For how many people is the first and last thought of the day about magnifying Christ among those who have never heard the gospel?

Schindler's List is a film based on a true story about a wealthy German businessman who begins to sympathize with the Jews during the Holocaust. He saves more than 1,300 Jews by hiring workers who are about to go into the death camps. At the end of the movie, after the war has ended, a large group of Jews gather to appreciate and thank him. He is given a ring engraved with a Hebrew saying from the Talmud: "whoever saves one life, saves the world entire." As he grips the hand of this precious Jewish man, he leans in and whispers, "I could have saved more. If I'd made more money...I threw away so much money...I didn't do enough! This car; I could have sold this car, I could have saved ten more people." He takes off a pin from his jacket, and looks at it in despair. "This pin...they would have given me one more." He begins to weep. "I could have got one more person and I didn't ... I didn't!" On the Day of Judgment, when all becomes clear, will I have regret related to how much time and resources I gave toward the salvation of souls? What will it be like when this age is over, and we meet the Lord to give an account of our lives? If heaven and hell are truly in the balance, won't we weep the same way? Let us weep now, and give all for the sake of the nations, while it is still today.

My goal is not to produce shame or guilt. Nor am I suggesting that every believer should be an apostle Paul or a Hudson Taylor. Notice that Jesus gives every believer a simple and unbelievably powerful way to engage in the Great Commission. He says *"pray earnestly"* (Matthew 9:38). Another way to be involved is found in Romans 10:15: "And how are they to preach unless they are sent?" This indicates that there is a massive support role to be played, and that this role is fundamental to the task. In the next chapter, I explore how God is raising up African believers who have this apostolic ambition and burden for the nations. I believe they will play a vital role in finishing the Great Commission. They need senders to rise up with the same burden. We are all in this together. It will take a global, multicultural, and diverse group of believers to complete the task. What is important is that you take the first step and make this great challenge your ambition.

1. Taylor, Howard. *The Spiritual Secret of Hudson Taylor*. New Kensington, PA: Whitaker House, 1996. 129.
2. Piper, John. *Let the Nations Be Glad!: The Supremacy of God in Missions.* 3rd ed. S.l.: Inter-Varsity Press, 2010. 179.
3. This term denotes those whom God foreknew and chose to be saved (Mark 13:20; Romans 8:33; 1 Peter 1:1). Both Arminians and Calvinists hold to this term with variation in its explanation and application as it relates to God's sovereignty and predestination.
4. Joshua Project. Accessed December 16, 2014. http://joshuaproject.net/.
5. Ali, Abdullah Yusuf. *The Meaning of the Holy Qur'an*. New ed. Beltsville, Md.: Amana Publications, 1997. All quotations.
6. Garrison, David. *Church Planting Movements: How God Is Redeeming a Lost World.* Midlothian, Va.: WIGTake Resources, 2004. 100.
7. White, James R. *What Every Christian Needs to Know about the Qur'an.* 135.
8. "Home." News of Persecuted Church. Aid for Christians Suffering Persecution. Accessed December 16, 2014. http://barnabasfund.org/.
9. Zwemer, Samuel Marinus. *Raymond Lull, First Missionary to the Moslems.* Kindle ed. New York: Funk & Wagnalls, 1902. All quotations about Raymond Lull are taken from here.
10. Pew Research Centers Religion Public Life Project RSS. October 6, 2009. Accessed December 16, 2014. http://www.pewforum.org/2009/10/07/mapping-the-global-muslim-population22/.
11. Pew Research Center.
12. Mandryk, Jason, and Johnstone, Patrick. *Operation World.* 7th ed. Colorado Springs, CO: InterVarsity Press, 2011. 22.

3

The Eleventh Hour Workers

Let's look more closely at the Great Commission passage in Matthew 28:18-20:

> And Jesus came and said to them, 'All authority in heaven and on earth has been given to me. Go therefore and make disciples of all nations, baptizing them in the name of the Father and of the Son and of the Holy Spirit, teaching them to observe all that I have commanded you. And behold, I am with you always, to the end of the age.'

We have already seen that Jesus' command was to make disciples of all the ethnic groups of the earth. That is his inheritance from the Father and he *must* have them. We know that this command was not just for the immediate disciples, because the window given to complete the task is *to the end of the age.* That hasn't come yet, and the apostles are dead, so the command must still live.

It is important to connect the promise "I am with you always" with the Great Commission. The command is to *go,* and the fact that he is with us is the empowerment to *do.* In a unique way, the promise of his presence is conditioned upon, and found within, the commandment to *go.* This language is very similar to the commissioning of Joshua and the Israelites. The Lord said to Joshua "Now therefore arise, *go* over this Jordan...No man shall be able to stand before you all the days of your life. Just as I was with Moses, so *I will be with you. I will not leave you* or forsake you...for the Lord your God is *with you wherever you go"* (Joshua 1:2, 5, 9). The presence of God would ensure the success of the Israelites in their mission.

Christ's Coming and the Great Commission

In Matthew 28, Jesus is saying that every nation must be reached, and that he will be with us to accomplish it until the end of the age. That brings up another crucial aspect of this mission. There is a dynamic link between the completion of Great Commission and the return of Christ. An almost identical idea is found in Matthew 24:14, "and this Gospel of the Kingdom will be preached as a witness to all nations and then the end will come." In this verse, two things *will* happen. First, the gospel of the kingdom will be preached as a witness to all nations. There is no demon or power in the earth that can stop this from happening. Jesus must have his lambs. Second, after this is accomplished, the end will come. It doesn't matter who has scoffed at his delay. It doesn't matter which governments are in place or who wants him to come back. It doesn't matter who is prepared and who is not. Ready or not, here he comes. We can expect Jesus to return when the Commission is fulfilled. Both will happen.

This eschatological expectation is a common backdrop in the preaching and mission of the apostles. Preaching in Jerusalem, Peter addressed the people of Israel: "Repent therefore, and turn back, that your sins may be blotted out, that times of refreshing may come from the presence of the Lord, and that he may send the Christ appointed for you, Jesus" (Acts 3:19-20). He is speaking to a Jewish audience (Acts 3:12) and the message is clear. Jesus will return when the Jewish people receive him as their Messiah. What is in view here is a national repentance that will usher in the eschaton (end of the age). In his epistle to the Romans, Paul tells us that the completion of the Great Commission will usher in this national repentance of Israel: "a partial hardening has come upon Israel, until the fullness of the Gentiles has come in" (Romans 11:25). When the full number of gentiles is reached, the partial hardening that is upon the nation of Israel as a result of their unbelief will be lifted.

This idea that the work of missions would speed up a national revival in Israel and ultimately the final return of Christ to Jerusalem was a driving factor in Paul's missionary spirit. If the ambition of Paul's life was to preach Christ where he had never been named, the zeal to accomplish this purpose was found in his longing for the return of Christ. It undergirded his entire ministry. He says to Timothy, "henceforth there is laid up for me the crown of righteousness, which the Lord the righteous judge, will award to me on that day, and not only to me but also to all who have loved his appearing" (2 Timothy 4:8).

On death row, Paul says that he is getting his crown because he has "loved", or as NIV translates it, "longed for" the appearing of Christ. How did Paul practically long for Christ to return? One answer is that he kept moving and pressing and going to new peoples and nations with the gospel. The way he contended for the salvation of the Jews was to labor for the full number of gentiles to come in. He knew the result of finishing the mission.

It is not just love for the lost that motivates missions, but also longing for Christ and his glory in the earth. When he comes, it means the restoration of the world and the exaltation of the glory of God. Jesus taught us to pray for and long for this, "Pray then like this, 'Our Father in heaven, hallowed be your name, your kingdom come, your will be done on earth as it is in heaven" (Matthew. 6:9-10).

What Hour Is It?

Jesus gave us a clue to discern the hour of his return. When every nation has a witness, when disciples are being made among every tribe, we will know the end is near. Where are we right now in this process? Some amazing predictions made by the world's leading missions organizations give us critical insight. Wycliffe, which has sent thousands of missionaries to the most unreached peoples, and is responsible for Bible translation work in numerous nations, recently projected that they will begin translation of the Bible in every known language by the year 2038. Their goal is to speed this time frame up, and actually accomplish this by the year 2025.[1] That is astounding. It is only within the last twenty years that we could even identify all the specific ethno-linguistic groups in the world.[2]

The Global Network of Mission Structures (GNMS) was initiated by the late Dr. Ralph Winter and organized by a group of missions strategists in 2005. The purpose was bringing together mission agencies from every sending country in the world to cooperate more effectively in finishing the task of reaching the remaining least-reached peoples. They held a conference in May 2010, in which missions leaders representing over 150,000 missionaries gathered. Projecting current trends in the missions movement around the world, they released the following statement:

> By the grace of God and the power of his Spirit, the GNMS as a vision and network commits itself and those it represents to doing whatever it takes to see the fulfillment of Revelation 5:9 in our generation. That we are very close to seeing this happen is the most exciting prospect of our time. But it also tells us that we are near to our Lord's second coming, and we must therefore hasten to work while it is day, for "the night is coming when no one can work" (John 9:4). Beyond any doubt, an unprecedented opportunity lies before us to see the Great Commission fulfilled. If current world conditions hold stable, it is very probable that this could happen in the next ten to fifteen years. Remarkably, this is almost exactly two thousand years after this assignment was given! Dare we not give it our all in this final stretch?[3]

It turns out that we are quite near to seeing the task finished. Part of the great rise in missions in the twentieth century was due to the Student Volunteer Movement chaired by a man named John R. Mott. In the decades between 1900 and 1940, over 20,000 students from universities in America decided to spend their lives to reach the interior lands of

Africa and Asia, dedicating themselves with the watch word, "the evangelization of the whole world in this generation".[4] They believed they could finish the Great Commission. Their movement fizzled out during the 1940s, but great progress was made in the interior lands of Africa and Asia, and their vision didn't die.

In the 50s and 60s, when communism took control of China and colonialism was falling apart in Africa and Asia, a new dawn in missions began. Western missionaries had to leave these countries in droves, but miracles took place. In the 1950s, China only had a Christian population of around 100,000. Western missionaries were forced to leave the Chinese Church on its own, and the prospect of evangelistic expansion looked bleak. Yet, when Chinese nationals took over the work, an explosion of growth took place. Today, the number of believers in China is between 100 and 200 million. Some estimate that 30,000 are being baptized every day in China.[5]

Africa has a similar story. Over the last 100 years, even more so in the last 60 (since the years of independence from colonialism), there has been massive growth in the African Church. Thousands of African men and women have taken up the gospel torch to win the lost. In 1900, there were 7.5 million believers in all of Africa. Today, there are more than 504 million people who call themselves Christians; 180 million Evangelical, 200 million Charismatic and Pentecostal.[6] Part of the reason for this amazing growth can be attributed to the fact that when colonialism was ousted, so was Western paternalism, and many churches came under the full responsibility of native believers. Protestant, Evangelical, and Pentecostal churches, fully lead by native believers, began multiplying exponentially across the landscape of Africa.

These churches were being planted and lead by common African men and woman, most of whom had little or no seminary training. Today, there is very little sign of slowing momentum. African churches led by African leaders continue to multiply and expand their influence.

At this same time, the Western missions movement was experiencing extraordinary development. Realizing that the gospel was already in every nation state in the world, but that there were still whole peoples isolated and cut off from the gospel, the discussion of people groups came to the forefront of the conversation. A major emphasis began to develop on reaching every tribe with the gospel. Missions organizations in the West began to shift focus and resources to reaching unreached tribes, and translating the Bible into rural tribal languages. According to Operation World, it is only within the last few decades that we have obtained a clear and comprehensive listing of all the world's people groups (approximately 16,350) and were able to identify the unreached tribes with accuracy.

There has been a clear acceleration of global evangelism and church planting in the last 100 years, especially in the last few decades. Today, the Church is actually coming close to achieving the lofty goal of the Student Volunteer Movement. Patrick Johnson, the founder of Operation World, writes of this extraordinary expansion in the last century:

> It is interesting how few of the world's peoples had been reached by 1800. The number of peoples reached had considerably increased by 1900, but even then, more than half the peoples of the world were still completely unreached. The dramatic change has been in the later part of this century (20th). Although many

> peoples are still unreached, the number is only a fraction of that of 100 years ago. The goal is attainable in our generation—if we mobilize prayer and effort and work together to disciple the remaining least-reached peoples.[7]

Ralph Winter also believed that reaching all the unengaged people groups could be directly on the horizon: "We can confidently speak of closure to this unreached peoples mission. There were an estimated 17,000 unreached peoples in 1976. Today there are an estimated 10,000 and a dynamic global movement now exists that is committed to establishing 'a church for every people.'"[8]

He was using a narrower definition of people groups at the time, but his point is relevant. It shows that in the last several decades, there has been a massive and successful increase in missions to the unreached, and it is still continuing today. The challenges of reaching these remaining groups are numerous, the biggest one being that many are dominated by Islam, but it seems clear that we are in the final hour of this work, and that a great opportunity lies before the Church to finish the Great Commission.

A Shift in World Missions

Why has there been such success in the unreached peoples task in the last several decades? One reason is that missions centers worldwide shifted their focus to reaching people groups and not just countries. Another major part of the answer is that, after World War II, missions entered a new phase. What was mostly a Western or Global North project began shifting to a multicultural worldwide effort. Pioneer missions work was increasingly being spearheaded by those in the Global South, as Asia, Africa, and South America surpassed North America and Europe in those claiming to be born again Christians.

Ben Naja describes this shift, and its implication for the missions movement in his book Releasing The Workers of the Eleventh Hour: The Global South and the Task Remaining: "At the beginning of the twentieth century, 94% of all Christians lived in the Global North. By the year 2000, 71% of all Christians were living in the Global South....this shift has dramatic implications for world missions."[9] Out of this harvest, God is raising a new, multicultural missions force: "The harvesters in the Global North are rapidly being joined by their fellow workers in the Global South. By the year 2025, four out of every five missionaries will be from the Global South."[10] Ralph Winter addressed this reality as well:

> God is moving throughout his global body to fulfill his promise to the nations in ways that we could not possibly have imagined 25 years ago. Thousands of new missionary recruits are no longer coming just from the West, but also from Asia, Africa, and Latin America—fruits of missionary movements—wholeheartedly embracing the peoples challenge of the Great Commission. More so than ever before missions is a global, cooperative movement. We have to be prepared for new partnerships, new insights, and new approaches by non Western mission structures.[11]

The Eleventh Hour Workers

I believe that we are in the season of the eleventh hour laborers. God is raising up a new missionary army in Africa and Asia to help bring in the end time harvest and usher in the return of the Lord.

> For the kingdom of heaven is like a master of a house who went out early in the morning to hire *laborers for his vineyard.* After agreeing with the laborers for a denarius a day, he sent them into his vineyard. And going on about the third hour he saw others standing idle in the marketplace, and to them he said, 'you go into the vineyard too, and whatever is right I will give to you.' So they went. Going out again about the sixth hour and the ninth hour, he did the same. And about *the eleventh hour* he went out and found others standing. And he said to them, 'Why do you stand here idle all day?' They said to him, 'because no one has hired us.' He said to them, '*You go into the vineyard too.*' And when evening came, the owner of the vineyard said to his foreman, 'Call the laborers and pay them their wages, beginning with the last, up to the first.' And when *those hired about the eleventh hour* came, each of them received a denarius. Now when those hired first came, they thought they would receive more, but each of them also received a denarius. And on receiving it they grumbled at the master of the house, saying, 'These last worked only one hour, and *you have made them equal to us* who have born the burden of the day and the scorching heat.' But he replied to one of them, 'Friend, I am doing you

> no wrong. Did you not agree with me for a denarius? Take what belongs to you and go. I choose to give to this last worker as I have given to you. Am I not allowed to do what I choose with what belongs to me? Or do you begrudge my generosity?' So the last will be first, and the first will be last. (Matthew 20:1-16)

This parable is fixed in the eschatological context of Matthew 19:28, "Jesus said to them, 'Truly, I say to you, in the new world, when the Son of Man will sit on his glorious throne, you who have followed me will also sit on twelve thrones, judging the twelve tribes of Israel.'" When the Son of Man comes and the earth is renewed, "everyone who has left houses or brothers or sisters or father or mother or children or lands, for my name's sake, will receive a hundredfold, and will inherit eternal life" (Matthew 19:29). This corresponds to the time when the "owner of the vineyard said to his foreman, 'Call the Laborers and pay them their wages.'"

It is also about the calling and rewarding of laborers who work in the vineyard; primarily the eleventh hour workers who will receive an equal payment to those called at other times of the day. Some are called, like Peter and the other apostles, in the early morning, some at the third hour, the sixth, the ninth, and then finally the eleventh hour, just before the master sends his foreman to pay the laborers. The eleventh hour workers are those whom the Lord will invite into his work during the last hour, or as seems clear from the context, at the end of the age.

Another part of the framework of this passage is that of discipleship, or following Christ. As we just saw in 19:28, this is about "you who have followed me" and those who have left "houses or brothers...for my name's sake." Leaving all to follow Christ had to do with entering his work, for his *name's sake*. When Jesus called Peter, Andrew, James, and John, in Matthew 4:18-22, he said, "follow me, and I will make you fishers of men." The text notes how they left all. Peter and Andrew "immediately...left their nets and followed him." and James and John "immediately...left the boat and their father and followed him."

In juxtaposition to this, the rich young ruler in Matthew 19 is called, but cannot cope with the challenge. He loves money more than Christ. Peter reminds Jesus, in contrast to the rich young ruler, "See, we have left everything and followed you. What then will we have?" At this point, Jesus affirms Peter's self denial, promises great reward in the age to come, and speaks a timeless parable to encourage all future laborers that there is an equal reward for those in every age who leave all to follow Christ and bring in the harvest.[12]

There is a correlation in this passage with John 4:35-38 as well. There, Jesus says, "the one who reaps is receiving wages and gathering fruit for eternal life...I sent you to reap that for which you did not labor. Others have labored, and you have entered into their labor." In John, the laborers are people who are called to work among the harvest, which is the multitudes of lost souls who need to be saved. They receive wages, just like the laborers of our parable in Matthew 20, and those wages include eternal life just as in Matthew 19:29. These two elements bring us to the right conclusion that this parable is about those called by God to labor among the lost and bring in the harvest of souls to the kingdom of God. Specifically, our parable deals with the laborers of the last hour, those called just before the return of the Lord. There will be an end time enlistment and the Lord wants us to know about it! But what does he want us to know about it?

The Sovereignty and Generosity of the Master

First, we are to see and acknowledge the sovereignty and generosity of the Master. He, the Lord of the harvest, is the one who hires laborers and sends workers into the vineyard. We see the same thing in Matthew 9:38, *"pray earnestly to the Lord of the harvest to send out laborers into his harvest."* It is God who calls! It is God who sends. He is free to choose whom he will to enter his work. Often, he chooses the most unlikely, like Peter and John who were uneducated men (Acts 4:13). Not only is he free to choose them, but also to lavish them with rewards according to his own will. The call is according to his grace and the reward is according to his generosity.

The Last Shall Be First and the First Shall Be Last

Second, he wants us to know that he will give the least likely candidates equal opportunity and reward. The parable is sandwiched with this expression, "the last will be first, and the first will be last" in Matthew 19:30 and 20:16, and directly in the middle. Chapter 20:8 says that the owner told his foreman to, "pay their wages, beginning with the last group to the first." Jesus is tempering his response to Peter. Even though he is one of the first to respond to the call, there will be others also, and they will obtain an equal reward. Just as his call to Peter was an act of grace and generosity, so also there would be others, in other generations, who would be invited. All harvesters of every generation who choose to follow him will be included in a special reward and have eternal life.

It is amazing to see how this might be relevant to what God is doing in our time by raising up laborers from the poorest countries on the earth. In Matthew 20:6-7, the master says to the laborers of the eleventh hour, "Why do you stand here idle all day?" "Because no one has hired us," they say to him. These are people who lack privilege and opportunity. Africa contains 32 of the 33 lowest ranking nations on the UN Human Development Index.[13] Unemployment in African countries can reach epidemic proportions, leaving most people to survive through local farming or any menial work that can possibly make them something to survive on. I once saw a billboard in Uganda, bringing awareness to unemployment, which said "265,000 young adult graduates from university are without employment." Many of these are passionate followers of Christ. Imagine if ten percent of them would give themselves to the harvest! That would be 26,500 new missionaries sent to the unreached, and that's just Uganda! There are multitudes of idle youth in Africa, and God is already enlisting them. Even as I am writing this, more are being called into the work of the gospel.

Dealing with Pride

Finally, the Lord deals with the very innate human issue of pride, which might exist in those who have worked longer and harder in the harvest, causing them to look down upon new laborers. Even though they are less privileged and have come in at the end of history, they are of no less value in their work than any of those who were hired at other times. Some feel that they have the corner on the missionary enterprise. Just like those who were hired earlier grumbled at the master, some people today would rather control how God moves, and through whom he works. Oh how this gets at the issue of pride and privilege! But this work is all for the glory of God.

He is free to bestow generosity and to call whom he wills for the sake of his name and glory. He is totally fair, he is totally free, and he wants total humility: "I choose to give to this last worker as I have given to you. Am I not allowed to do what I choose with what belongs to me? Or do you begrudge my generosity?"

There is a warning here, not to minimize what God is doing with native missionaries in Asia and Africa, but to treat them as equals in the work of the Great Commission. Any discrimination and entitlement that may creep up in the hearts of those who come from more privileged backgrounds, or from more well established missions organizations, should be done away with. We must refuse the temptation of pride. God has called these native missionaries into the vineyard, and they are worthy of their wages.

It is important to realize that the eleventh hour workers are not replacing those called before them. They are joining them in the work. Just as the Church fathers were building on the labors of the Apostles, or many believers in Africa today are building on the labors of David Livingstone. The point is not replacement, the point is cooperation. By highlighting the importance of missionaries from the Global South, I am not implying that Global North missionaries should give up all foreign missions work and be replaced. If anything, missionaries from every nation represent the eleventh hour laborers. I am showing, however, that there is a need to work in full partnership with the missionaries of the Global South, and to consider how God has called us to help empower them for the work. We need to see them as full partners, not as dependents. Operation World states in their section on Africa that,

> The missionary force is increasingly African and multi-continental and less Western. Much sensitivity and humility is required for effective ministry that reaches the unevangelized and defers to the maturity and vision of the growing African Church... But today's realities mean that ministry in Africa can largely be led by Africans, supported by expatriates. Pray for unity and fellowship that transcend all social and cultural barriers within mission agencies, among agencies themselves, and between the indigenous churches and agencies.[14]

In other words, we are in a season of partnership which requires humility. Acknowledging equality always requires meekness. Jesus wanted us to know that laboring in the vineyard in the eleventh hour would require humility.

So, what is the role of the Church in the Global North? Are we putting off responsibility by highlighting the role of native missionaries? There is great responsibility for the Church in the West, especially the American Church. America continues to be the leader in sending cross-cultural missionaries, and it should continue to do so. Its Church, whether for good or for bad, carries great influence in the direction and culture of the Church worldwide. The Western Church has the most experience and the most intellectual centers in Christianity. It also has the majority of the money needed to fulfill the commission of Jesus. I would say that our role has simply changed. Now that we are joined by a multitude of laborers from the Global South, we need to focus on strategic ways of equipping, funding, and serving native missionary movements.

Effectiveness of Missionaries from the Global South

Global South believers are generally very effective in planting churches and evangelizing among unreached people groups near them. Ben Naja, who is himself a seasoned Western missionary in North Africa, identifies seven areas where the workers from the Global South are closer to unreached peoples than those living in the Global North: geographically, culturally, linguistically, economically, educationally, sociologically, and missiologically.[15] This proximity gives them a great advantage in reaching their neighboring tribes with the gospel.

African missionaries are willing to go to the nations with a fraction of the support that it costs to maintain a Global North missionary. It takes between $200 and $400 per month to support a native missionary. This is quite a contrast with the average American or European missionary who will need between $2,000 and $6,000 per month. They need this amount to maintain a Western standard of living among the people they are trying to reach, and to pay for frequent international travel. Often, the economic divide between the first world missionary and the third world people group he or she is trying to reach becomes an inescapably difficult barrier for modern Western missionaries. The native African missionary completely avoids the dilemma, reaching people from his own socio-economic background.

We should not overlook the linguistic factors either. For the average Western missionary, it might take years to learn a foreign language. Languages are difficult for Americans because they usually don't have to learn more than one. Operation World recognizes the specific challenge of Africa in this area: "A high degree of commitment and sacrifice will be required to reach present pioneer areas where conditions are sometimes very hard. In some cases missionaries will need to learn two to four languages before they can reach the least-reached."[16]

For the African missionary, this is simply not as great of a challenge. It is not uncommon for an average person from Africa to speak three or four languages despite his educational level. This knack for languages is forced on the people of African countries that contain multiple (sometimes hundreds) of languages.

One of our *Send56* missionaries comes from a town in North Kenya containing unreached peoples. He is a former Muslim from a tribe called the Borana. The Borana are less than 5% Christian as a whole, but the gospel seems to be spreading rapidly among them. They have a neighboring tribe called the Garreh, who are completely unreached and unengaged (no missionary working among them) fundamentalist Muslims. The Garreh are related to both the Borana and the Somali peoples, and they have maintained both of these languages. This Borana missionary expressed to me his excitement and vision for planting churches among the unreached Garreh, with whom he shares a language.

Another great advantage for native missionaries is in their lack of political baggage. In Islamic areas, Western missionaries enter a politically charged atmosphere where they are viewed with great suspicion. Of course the perception that the West is anti-Islamic, and even at war with Islam, is a great hindrance to witness. In many places, Christianity has been effectively labeled as foreign, or "the white man's religion." For obvious reasons, the native missionary completely avoids this label, and is able to assimilate into Islamic culture with very little suspicion and no political baggage.[17]

Many wonderful and groundbreaking missionaries from the Global North have spilt their blood so that the African Church could be where it is today. Western missionaries continue to play an integral part in reaching Africa and the world. The wonderful news is that now there is a new generation of missionaries, made up of thousands of indigenous African believers, who are ready to take the torch of the gospel into the remaining tribes that have not yet been reached. This multicultural missions force, made up of passionate believers from all over the world, working in partnership to bring in the end time harvest, might just be the eleventh hour laborers.

1. Creson, Bob. *Vision 2025 Rapidly Accelerating the Pace of Bible Translation.* August, 2006. Accessed January 9, 2015. http://www.missionfrontiers.org/pdfs/28-4-cresson. pdf.
2. Mandryk, Jason, and Patrick Johnstone. *Operation World. 7th ed.* Colorado Springs, CO: InterVarsity Press , 2011. 25.
3. *Global Network of Mission Structures.* Accessed January 8, 2015. http://gnms.net/.
4. Winter, Ralph. *Perspectives Reader. S.l.*: William Carey Library, 2013. 281-283.
5. Garrison, David. *Church Planting Movements: How God Is Redeeming a Lost World.* Midlothian, Va.: WIGTake Resources, 2004. 49.
6. Mandryk, Jason, and Patrick Johnstone. *Operation World.* 33.
7. Winter, Ralph. *Perspectives.* 217.
8. Winter, Ralph. *Perspectives.* 517.
9. Naja, Ben. *Releasing the Workers of the Eleventh Hour: The Global South and the Task Remaining.* Pasadena, Calif.: William Carey Library Publishers, 2007. n.p.
10. Naja, Ben. *Releasing the Workers of the Eleventh Hour.* n.p.
11. Winter, Ralph. *Perspectives.* 523.
12. This does not mean that all people are given the same reward in the age to come. The equal reward for all is eternal life. Jesus is showing Peter that all who follow him and join the work will be equally rewarded in the age to come with eternal life. This does not mean the quality of that life will not be different. Other passages clearly teach differing degrees of reward in the age to come.
13. Mandryk, Jason, and Patrick Johnstone. *Operation World.* 31.
14. Mandryk, Jason, and Patrick Johnstone. *Operation World.* 38.
15. Naja, Ben. *Releasing the Workers of the Eleventh Hour.* 28.
16. Mandryk, Jason, and Patrick Johnstone. *Operation World.* 38.
17. I am generalizing for the sake of making a point. There are cases where certain tribes or nations will have adversarial relations to other tribes or nations within Africa.

4

Life Hangs on a Word

All of life hangs on a word. Hebrews tells us that God "upholds the universe by the word of his power." The word of God is the agent of creation, restoration, and salvation. In the beginning, God caused the universe to explode into existence by his word…"let there be light."

> For the word of God is living and active, sharper than any two-edged sword, piercing to the division of soul and of spirit, of joints and of marrow, and discerning the thoughts and intentions of the heart. And no creature is hidden from his sight, but all are naked and exposed to the eyes of him to whom we must give account. (Hebrews 4:12–13)

In this passage, the word is personified; no one is hidden from "his sight." The same idea is found in John 1:1 and 1:14, where we find out that the second person of the Trinity is the

Word of God, and that at one time, for the sake of salvation, "the Word became flesh and dwelt among us." Now, that word is being made known as the means of salvation, to the ends of the earth, through the proclamation of all disciples. Eternal life is in his word, and the word is conveyed through preaching. Preaching must be central in mission because the word is central. The word is Christ.

After rising from the dead, Jesus commanded the disciples, "Go into all the world and *proclaim the gospel* to the whole creation. Whoever believes and is baptized will be saved" (Mark 16:15-16). The connection is clear that preaching is necessary for the nations to receive salvation, and that this preaching is the mission of the Church. Yet, there is a great temptation in this current cultural era to make missions another humanitarian effort and not a gospel and discipleship effort. Many today think of missions in terms of social justice or humanitarianism. The large disparity between people who live in affluent Western countries and those living in third world countries raises a natural desire to help the poor, but not necessarily to see salvation of souls. There is a broad desire to "serve", but this is too often construed to be the apostolic mandate.

The message of secular humanism, which is so ingrained in today's Western culture, says "do not encroach on another world view because all views are equal." Increasingly, anyone who preaches Christ is labeled as being ignorant and judgmental. For this reason, it is a great temptation to take an easier road and hide the gospel behind good deeds in the name of missions, so as not to offend the world by preaching a message with truth claims and repentance. The Church must not cave to this pressure. Anything less than a full proclamation of the kingdom of God and salvation through Christ is not the real thing.

Missions is a term that can easily absorb whatever definition people want it to have. Do most believers understand missions as the apostolic mandate given by Christ to the Church, to "go" and "preach the gospel" and "make disciples" among all tribes and nations? I think that many people just don't know that is what it is supposed to mean. For many, missions just means reaching out within different cultures or helping poor people, and maybe, in the minds of many, it means evangelism in general. It is good to define the biblical mandate, and narrow the meaning, so that we get our priorities straight.

The Mission of the Church

We have already looked at Matthew 28:18-20 and Mark 16:15-16. Let's add to this Luke 24:46-48 and Acts 1:8. In these four parallel accounts, Jesus gives a direct commission to the disciples; a mandate to preach and to disciple the nations of the earth until he returns. From this it is rightly derived that the Church has a mission to fulfill, and it is hardly contestable what that mission is. His word must go out, through preaching and teaching, to the ends of the earth, so that people can turn from false worship and idolatry, give due glory to God through Christ, and be saved from eternal condemnation. Rich and poor alike have scorned the name of the one true God, and the only way for healing is for rich and poor alike to repent and turn to Yahweh through Jesus, and receive their blood-bought forgiveness by faith.

Kevin DeYoung and Greg Gilbert give us their biblical definition in <u>What is the Mission of the Church: Making Sense</u>

of Social Justice, Shalom, and the Great Commission: "The Mission of the Church is to go into the world and make disciples by declaring the gospel of Jesus Christ in the power of the Spirit and gathering these disciples into churches, that they might worship the Lord and obey his commands now and in eternity to the glory of God the Father."[1]

I agree with this statement, but also further specify that missions is the apostolic mandate, given by Jesus, to do these things among *unreached* peoples. Some have termed my narrower definition as "frontier" missions, or "pioneer" missions. I like the term "apostolic mandate," because I believe frontier missions is essentially the command Jesus gave to his apostles after the resurrection, and is the primary missionary call. I don't discredit the broader view above, which would include going out and making disciples in your neighborhood. But there must be a biblical category in our minds for this narrow focus, which is to go to the unreached.

Many would agree that Paul should be taken as a model missionary, one who had received the apostolic mandate from Jesus. In Romans 15, he gives one of the clearest and most definitive examples of what the Great Commission is in reference to his own ministry:

> Because of the grace given me by God to be a minister of Christ Jesus to the Gentiles in the priestly service of the gospel of God, so that the offering of the Gentiles may be acceptable, sanctified by the Holy Spirit. In Christ Jesus, then, I have reason to be proud of *my work for God*. For I will not venture to speak of anything except what Christ has accomplished through me *to bring the Gentiles to obedience—by word and deed*, by the power of signs and wonders, *by the*

> *power of the Spirit* of God—so that from Jerusalem and all the way round to Illyricum I have fulfilled the ministry of the gospel of Christ; and thus *I make it my ambition to preach* the gospel, *not where Christ has already been named,* lest I build on someone else's foundation, but as it is written, 'Those who have never been told of him will see, and those who have never heard will understand.' (Romans 15:15-21)

Paul talks about his "work for God," which he does as a "minister of Christ Jesus," to bring "the Gentiles to obedience." In Romans 1:5, we see that this is the "obedience of faith" in the gospel of Christ. He gives a crucial direction for how the Lord wants the mission carried out; "by word and deed." The word is given primacy, "I make it my ambition to preach the gospel." The *deeds* of this verse are not just any aspect of charity or service, rather Paul is referring to the "signs and wonders, by the power of the spirit of God" found in verse 19. The Great Commission done right is done by word with deeds that display the power of the living God and confirm the truth of the gospel. Finally, the ministry of word and deed is aimed at "those who have never been told of him, and, those who have never heard." In Paul's biblically-based understanding of the commission that Jesus left to the Church, missions was not just proclaiming the gospel in the power of the Spirit and making disciples, it was also doing this among people groups that were unreached.

By Word and Deed

The word with deeds of power is the way of the gospel. Jesus sent out the disciples in Acts 1:8, "But you will receive power when the Holy Spirit has come upon you, and you will be my witnesses…to the end of the earth." The Holy Spirit gave life and power to the word of the disciples, and made it effective in bringing the elect to salvation. In 1 Corinthians 2:4, Paul says, "my speech and my message were not in plausible words of wisdom, but in demonstration of the Spirit and of power." That is how Paul thought missions should be accomplished, and for a very good reason, "that your faith might not rest in the wisdom of men but in the power of God." If missions is accomplished by word and deed, Jesus will be glorified, and not the wisdom of men:

> To this end we always pray for you, that our God would make you worthy of his calling and may fulfill every resolve for good and *every work of faith by his power, so that the name of our Lord Jesus may be glorified* in you, and you in him, according to the grace of our God and the Lord Jesus Christ. (2 Thessalonians 1:11-12)

The Gospel of Mark in particular highlights that the ministry of Jesus was composed of both preaching and demonstrations, whether by healings or casting out demons. It also shows that Jesus expected that type of ministry would be continued through his disciples, and not just the twelve, but also through all who would believe. The way Paul did missions, as we have just seen, is the way that Jesus did it, and the way he wants it to be done in general. Let's start with Mark 1:14-39:

> Jesus came into Galilee, proclaiming the gospel of God,…

...And he healed many who were sick with various diseases, and cast out many demons....

...And he said to them, "let us go on to the next towns, that I may preach there also, for that is why I came out." And he went throughout all Galilee, preaching in their synagogues and casting out demons.

Jesus launches his ministry, coming out of the wilderness empowered by the Holy Spirit, with a proclamation. In most cases in this Gospel, preaching is followed by casting out demons, as in Mark 1:39. In chapters 3 and 6, we see him transfer this work to the disciples:

> And he appointed twelve (whom he also named apostles) so that they might be with him and he might send them out *to preach* and have authority to *cast out demons*. (Mark 3:14-15)
>
> And he called the twelve and began to send them out two by two, and gave them authority over unclean spirits....So they went out and proclaimed that people should repent. And they cast out many demons and anointed with oil many who were sick and healed them. (Mark 6:7, 12-13)

It is undeniable that the ministry of Jesus, in proclamation of the gospel and in power, was to be continued through the apostles. It is also clear that this was the primary way that people would be brought into the kingdom. But what about our current generation?

In Mark 16:15, Jesus extended the ministry of proclamation beyond the towns of Israel to "all the world," but this still does not necessarily extend this missionary task to anyone other than the disciples. However, the next phrase does: "and these signs will accompany those who believe." If this mission is only for the twelve, it hardly makes sense to say this. But if Jesus is widening the work, as I believe he is doing here, to all who believe, it makes perfect sense: "In my name they will cast out demons; they will speak in new tongues…they will lay their hands on the sick and they will recover" (Mark 16:17-18). This type of ministry is not just for the apostles, but for all who believe. Gospel preaching, with signs and wonders following, is a broad missionary mandate that applies to our time as well. Mark ends with the ascension of Jesus in verse 19, "they went out and preached everywhere, while the Lord worked with them and confirmed the message by accompanying signs."[2]

I do not think there is any reason to believe that the strategy the Lord Jesus gave to the disciples in the Gospel of Mark, and the one employed by Paul in Romans 15, has changed. We don't need new gimmicks to be relevant in today's world, we need the same old word and power of God. We must get back to apostolic preaching, with demonstration of the Spirit's power, as the way of the Lord in missions.

There is a temptation to take what I am saying and imagine a televangelist or gospel crusader, but that is not my main reference point. I am picturing a humble servant of Christ visiting huts in the wilderness of Africa and, after sharing the gospel with a family, offering to pray in the name of Jesus for the sick of that household who may not have been able to visit the hospital. Preaching with miracles can be done by anyone who believes the gospel. It is important to remember that most of the world has very little access to good medical services. In many parts of the world, there are no options for those who are suffering debilitating diseases. Healing the sick is a vital aspect of ministry in the world.

Preaching, praying for the sick, and casting out demons can be done with or without a pulpit, with or without big crowds. I have no reason to minimize the importance of preaching to masses of people—Jesus ministered to crowds often, and it is important for those who have that gifting—but he also ministered to a Samaritan woman at a well, and brought deliverance to a lonely and tormented demon-possessed man in a graveyard. Many times, miracle stories are not found in the crowds, but in hidden and obscure places where servants of Christ find themselves available for God to use. I am not promoting a hyper-faith that assumes every person that is prayed for will be healed in this age. God chooses who will be healed, as we become vessels of faith.

A woman in a Muslim African village gave her life to Jesus when a group of Christians from her tribe shared the gospel with her. Her husband was a strong Muslim who lost his job as a police officer because he was not willing to shave his Islamic beard. He would rather lose his job and remain faithful to Islam. His mother shared the same compound with them, and fell deathly ill. She was also a Muslim who openly practiced witchcraft. The same humble men who had shared the gospel with his wife came to visit the man's home and shared Jesus, that he is real and has the power to heal. Having noticed a difference in his wife since she confessed Christ, and broken down by his mother's imminent death, the man allowed this group of believers to come in and pray over her. As a group, they stepped into the dark hut and laid hands on this woman whose condition was obviously deteriorating. The presence of God filled the room and the woman miraculously recovered.

So great was the testimony of this woman's healing that others decided to follow Christ, including her son who was a staunch Muslim. In fact, the entire family came to Christ. I visited their rural home soon after this occurred. As we drove into the compound of a few separate grass-thatched huts, we were greeted by an exuberant and shining elderly woman. When I got out of the vehicle, she grabbed my face and kissed me! She was so vibrant and alive, ecstatic that Christians had come to visit them. I could hardly believe this woman was recently dying and had for a year been confined to her bed! The impact that this miracle had on the community was astounding. Practically the entire Muslim village was interested in hearing more about Christ.

Whats the Difference?

It is this word and power that separates missions from any other worldly, humanistic solution to global problems. The problem of the world is not a lack of money, resources, or good healthcare, but that the nations have rebelled against God. Jesus sent us to tell the nations: "now he commands all people everywhere to repent, because he has fixed a day on which he will judge the world in righteousness by a man whom he has appointed; and of this he has given assurance to all by raising him from the dead" (Acts 17:31-32).

It is the word of God that makes the Church different than the United Nations. American Idol raised millions of dollars in one day to aid Africa, but none of that money helped solve the main problems of sin and separation from God. Only the word of Christ can remove the veil that keeps multitudes in spiritual darkness.[3] Only the word of Christ can deliver souls from the snare of the devil and break the chains of bondage over multitudes. Biblical missions is messengers sent to proclaim the gospel of God; ambassadors entrusted with the saving and powerful word of Christ. There is still great need to send out more laborers whose primary work is proclamation and disciple-making among the unreached. Romans 10 is an clarion call to the body of Christ, to raise up and fund preachers of the gospel to the nations:

> For everyone who calls on the name of the Lord will be saved. How then will they call on him in whom they have not believed? And how are they to believe in him of whom they have never heard? And *how are they to hear without someone preaching*? And *how are they to preach unless they are sent*? As it is written: 'How beautiful are the feet of those who preach the good news!' But they have not all obeyed the gospel. For Isaiah says, 'Lord, who has believed what he has heard from us?' So faith comes from hearing, and hearing through the word of Christ. (Romans 10:14-17)

Salvation has been made available "to all who call upon the name of the Lord." But the faith or belief that would cause a person to call upon the Lord comes through hearing the gospel: "How are they to believe in whom they have never heard?...faith comes from hearing, and hearing through the word of Christ." How will people hear this eternal and saving word? Through "those who preach the good news."

Discipleship

In Acts 19, Paul takes twelve men and begins to disciple them in a rented hall called the school of TyrannTyrannusus.

After two years of daily teaching and training, "all the residents of Asia heard the word of the Lord, both Jews and Greeks" (Acts 19:10). Missions is a discipleship effort, which includes training and sending those who have been entrusted with a weighty, world-changing, life-saving word.

Paul very closely followed the model of Jesus here; twelve are taken into a core group, taught, and then sent out to teach. It is probable that Timothy was among the group of disciples in Ephesus, and it seems this was essential to his later pastoral work. It was critical to Paul that the word he passed on to Timothy would continue to be shared with other faithful stewards, "and what you have heard from me in the presence of many witnesses entrust to faithful men who will be able to teach others also" (2 Timothy 2:2). The word needs the right vessel to proclaim it, and for that reason, discipleship is a key aspect of missions.

It is within the context of community, discipline, prayer, fasting, and the study of Scripture that someone is prepared for the challenges that will come on account of that word. Paul's method of training in the Hall of Tyrannus was not simply academic, although he was lecturing around four hours daily. It was also practical. Within a two-year period, the word was being preached throughout Asia, presumably by the twelve (and others) that Paul was working with. If study is not coupled with practical application, it is often lost on the student, especially in missions. The pastor or missionary should be nurtured and taught the word by example. They must be immersed in a community of brethren pursing the Lord with wholeheartedness, where character is tested and shaped and where he or she learns to walk with discipline, integrity, and humility. Sitting in class is only part of what is needed. The missionary must learn to love, forgive, experience grace, and grow in prayer and the knowledge of God. Living together in community accelerates all of these areas of growth, and for this reason training institutes like the Hall of Tyranus are vital to mission work.

In *Send56*, I have witnessed the power of discipleship. In our training schools called MAP, the school of Missions and Prayer, student missionaries wake up early in the morning and engage in personal Bible study. They have classes throughout the week, emphasizing character development and theology, and sharing the gospel with Muslims. Throughout the week, they spend time in the 24/7 prayer room, which is part of each missions base. They regularly serve orphans, and every weekend they travel to different villages and preach the gospel. They learn the power of forgiving one another, loving one another, and walking together in a common goal. One of my favorite times at our missions base is sharing the Lord's Supper. Each week, the whole school gathers for a meal that includes communion. They worship, meditate on Christ's gift, and fellowship together.

After two years, we see lives transformed. Many students have expressed that they have a deeper relationship with the Lord. They can understand the Bible, share their faith, and make disciples. Their hearts are gripped with a burden to preach the gospel in the nations at whatever cost. During our corporate prayer meetings, I have witnessed students falling on their faces, groaning with tears, asking God to send them to the lost. I have never been more convinced than I am today that discipleship is crucial to sending out prepared gospel laborers.

Entrusted with the Word

The gospel was no light thing for the apostles. Paul said it was "entrusted" to him (2 Timothy 1:12). It was something to be stewarded, "I became a minister according to the stewardship from God that was given to me for you, to make the word of God fully known,...Him we proclaim" (Colossians 1:25-28). He "was appointed a preacher" (2 Timothy 1:12). Timothy was too. Paul tells him, "Follow the pattern of sound words that you have heard from me in faith and love that are in Christ Jesus. By the Holy Spirit...guard the good deposit *entrusted* to you" (2 Timothy 1:14). The word is entrusted to those who will preach it in the world, because it is the hope of the world. It is that "which God, who never lies, promised before the ages began and at the proper time manifested in his word through the preaching with which I have been *entrusted* by the command of God our Savior" (Titus 1:2-3).

The word of Christ causes conflict. It says of Stephen that, "They could not withstand the wisdom and the Spirit with which he was speaking." So they stoned him to death (Acts 7:58). To Stephen, the declaration of the gospel was a higher priority than the preservation of his own life. But there is no power that can stop the mighty proclamation of Christ. Not even prison can stop the living word. Writing from a cell, Paul tells us, "I am suffering, bound with chains as a criminal. But the word of God is not bound" (2 Timothy 2:9).

Trials are inevitable for those who speak the truth, but the Lord promised to guard the carriers of his word and preserve them for his eternal kingdom. Jesus knew that we would have to preach in hostile territory, so he promised, "I am with you always, to the end of the age" (Matthew 28:20). Paul makes it clear that it was by divine protection, "so that through me the message might be fully proclaimed and all the Gentiles might hear it. So I was rescued from the lion's mouth" (2 Timothy 4:17–18). At another point he says, "I am convinced that he is able to guard until that Day what has been entrusted to me" (2 Timothy 1:12). The Lord has entrusted his word to men and women of faith, sent forth into the world, even as Jesus was sent forth:

> For I have given them the words that you gave me, and they have received them and have come to know in truth that I came from you;...As you sent me into the world, so I have sent them into the world....
>
> ...'I do not ask for them only, but also for those who will believe in me through their word.' (John 17:8,18,20)

The Priority of the Word

Salvation came into the world through Jesus, and now goes out to the world through preaching.

This means that the hope of the nations is not found in the bread of the earth. It is found in the bread of heaven, which is the word of Christ. What a tragedy when the Church fails to realize this and neglects to send out preachers! Millions of dollars are appropriated toward the next big handout instead of the next big send-out. We are mobilizing food, clothing, and medical personnel, but how many preachers are we mobilizing and "how are they to preach unless they are sent?" Multitudes are left under the dominion of demons. Countless people are being left with powerful mental strongholds that can only be pulled down by weapons not of this world.

Paul says, "the weapons of our warfare are not of the flesh but have divine power to destroy strongholds. We destroy arguments and every lofty opinion raised against the knowledge of God" (2 Corinthians 10:4-5).What does Paul mean here? How is he destroying arguments? I think it is in the same way he tells Timothy, "preach the word; be ready in season and out of season; reprove, rebuke, and exhort, with complete patience and teaching....do the work of an evangelist, fulfill your ministry" (2 Tim 4:2-5). I wonder how many millions have fallen into hell because the Church has not put that first. People who were ripe to hear, but no one told them, no one was sent, and now they are fallen from the vine never to return. Oh, how we need to pray for laborers, and to ask God for beautiful feet! "How beautiful are the feet of those who preach the good news!" (Romans 10:15).

I am certainly not devaluing charity, humanitarian effort, or the labors of thousands of wonderful Christians who have served the poor and broken.

> Religion that is pure and undefiled before God, the Father, is this; to visit orphans and widows in their affliction, and to keep oneself unstained from the world. (James 1:27)
>
> If a brother or sister is poorly clothed and lacking in daily food, and one of you says to them, 'Go in peace, be warm and filled,' without giving them the things needed for the body, what good is that? So also faith by itself, if it does not have works, is dead. (James 2:15-17)

Good works can help preach the gospel. Good works confirm the gospel. Good works glorify God. Good works are the outworking of the love that Jesus demands we have for our neighbor. God has enough resources to fund hospitals, orphanages, schools, and to send out the laborers to preach. It is not *either* charity or preaching. It is impossible to calculate the good that Christian missionaries have done all over Africa to serve the poor and needy, to educate, and to bring better healthcare services in the name of Christ. No one has served Africa better than faithful Christians, or made life better for its people. This is not a question of charity or no charity; it is a question of priority.

> In today's cultural climate, where the accolades come quickly to those with humanitarian strategies and the opprobrium falls fast on those with evangelistic concerns, it is even more imperative that we keep the main thing the main thing. The danger is real. If we do not share the gospel—with words!—the story will not be told.[4]

There are devastating consequences for the Church and the world when we do not put the word first.

God Will Not Be at the Center

First, God's worth and centrality will be undervalued, and man will be exalted to first place. This is devastating for humanity. We must identify and dismantle the lie that God's glory is less valuable than man's temporary well being. Man cannot and will not ever be well, apart from making God's glory the center of life. When we remove God from first place, we remove the foundation of our intrinsic value and gut the means of eternal joy. Every endeavor to help man without reconciling man to God through Christ, the only mediator, is simply another form of secular humanism and will ultimately end in ruin.

This does not mean we should only help the needy in relationship to verbal witness, rather it means we should never help them exclusively without it. People have intrinsic worth because they are created by God, in his image. Human beings are valuable because they reflect the worth and glory of God, and he wanted them to exist. They are valuable precisely because they are the objects of God's love. This is in stark contrast to a purely naturalistic worldview which cannot ascribe any actual intrinsic value to a human being. Under naturalism, we would only value someone according to special attributes they might posses in themselves, whether beauty, strength, talents, riches, intellect, power, etc. This is exactly what a godless world values in people. It does not value the intrinsic beauty of God's image in both strong and weak. Naturalism would love to solve the problem of pain and suffering, and seeks to do so for the sake of empathy and general wellbeing, but it cannot, nor will it ever be able to, give worth and value to human beings.

When we put God's glory first, which is displayed so supremely in the gospel, humanity is served best. For if we try to love people apart from the gospel, we actually end up leaving them in ruin. We leave them helpless to the temptations of sin and the influence of the enemy. We root them in temporal fixes while their soul continues to perish not knowing the source of eternal joy. Happiness is not in money, or power, or physical pleasure. It is in knowing the source of life *himself*. In order to be healed, people must glorify God and not man—so in order to love well, we must exalt God and not man.

Humanity's problems are deeper than the skin. We have a worship problem:

> For although they knew God, they did not honor him as God or give thanks to him, but became futile in their thinking, and their foolish hearts were darkened. Claiming to be wise they became fools, and exchanged the glory of the immortal God for images resembling mortal man and birds and animals and creeping things. (Romans 1:21-23)

This failure of worship resulted in idolatry, the worship of man in place of God, and marks humanity's descent into sin and destruction: "Therefore God gave them up in the lust of their hearts to impurity, to the dishonoring of their bodies among themselves, because they exchanged the truth about God for a lie and worshiped and served the creature rather than the creator, who is blessed forever! Amen" (Romans 1:24-25).

Here, the purpose of the gospel shines strongest. The gospel delivers mankind from idolatry by glorifying God's mercy in the propitiatory work of Christ, while at the same time removing mankind's boasting in self. Because righteousness is a free gift and "not of ourselves," we are saved through a posture of self abasement, whereby this gift, received through humble faith, results in renewed praise that redounds to the glory of God. It is not what *we* have done, but what he has done for us. Faith in the gospel says what humans stopped saying after the fall—*thank You!* All boasting and glory returns to God.

It is important to understand that the gospel is not about man first; it is about God first. It is not primarily God acting on behalf of man, but God acting on behalf of God (which is also an act on behalf of man, because it is in his character to love us). If it were any other way, God would not be good.

Imagine if God allowed man to be in the center. What would result? The answer is observed throughout the history of humanity. Pride wins, lust wins, covetousness wins. The most loving thing that God can do for the human race is to uphold what is most lovely, worthy, and good—himself. If God allows humanity to be in the center, infinite love will not win, justice will not win, goodness will not win. Someone in the center without infinite virtue and infinite power to uphold that virtue leads to absolute desolation. But if God puts God in first place, infinite virtue and beauty and love and goodness will conquer. That is what God is doing through the gospel—restoring himself to first place.

Souls Will be Forfeited

Second, when the Church fails to prioritize the word in missions, people end up putting their trust in temporal fixes without dealing with the weight of their own sin and impending eternal judgment. We need to realize that material temporal fixes are only material and temporal, and cannot deliver the soul of a man from his separation from God because of sin. Jesus says, "for what will it prophet a man if he gains the whole world and forfeits his soul?" (Matthew 16:26). Is it possible to help people and not try to deliver them from hell? If we do not put the word first, we are doing just that. We need to be more concerned about the eternal destiny of a man than for his temporary wellbeing. This is why the word must be the first priority in missions; not health care, education, social services or anything else. K.P. Yohannan of Gospel for Asia gives us the same warning:

> To look into the sad eyes of a hungry child or see the wasted life of a drug addict is only to see the evidence of Satan's hold on this world. He is the ultimate enemy of mankind, and he will do everything within his considerable power to kill and destroy people. But to try and fight this terrible enemy with physical weapons is like fighting tanks with stones...The answer lies in our basic understanding of what missions work is all about. There is nothing wrong with charitable acts—but they are not to be confused with preaching the gospel. Feeding programs can save a man from dying of hunger. Medical aid can prolong life and fight disease. Housing projects can make this temporary life more comfortable—but only the gospel of Jesus Christ can save a soul from a life of sin and an eternity in hell![5]

The word must be first, even before humanitarianism, because it goes to the root and addresses eternal issues. Imagine a doctor visiting a rural people drinking from a contaminated well. He treats infections caused from using the water to bathe, and he gives people drugs to treat stomach viruses caused by drinking the water. How would you feel if the doctor refused to tell the people not to drink from the well, even though he knows that it is the source of their diseases? That is exactly what is happening when we put man first. We are not treating the root of the problem—that they have ceased to glorify God. Someone needs to tell them to stop drinking contaminated water, and to start drinking from the right source. That is what preachers do. They tell people to drink from the right source. It is good to dress the wounds and clean the infections, but it is vital to tell the people the source of the problem, and how to fix it. They need to repent, which means to turn away from what they are currently doing, and receive the free gift of living, cleansing water. Once again, I refer to DeYoung and Gilbert:

> Since hell is real, we must never think alleviating earthly suffering is the most loving thing we can do....The doctrine of hell reminds us that the greatest need of every person will not be met by the United Nations or Habitat for Humanity or the United Way. It is only through Christian witness, through proclamation of Christ crucified, that the worst thing in all the world will not fall on all those in the world.[6]

Social and Cultural Transformation Will Be Hindered

Finally, failing to prioritize the word actually hinders social and cultural transformation. Eternal salvation is not the only result of the lost hearing the word and believing. Prioritizing the word also leads to the cultural transformation and prosperity we long to see in our fallen world in the here and now. When the gospel takes root, many of the issues that cause poverty and disease are inevitably defeated.

The Karamojong have a philosophy that teaches them to value the life of cattle more than that of human beings. Theft and murder are common parts of their culture, and have been for many years. I had the amazing privilege of going to preach the word of God to some of these people. The Bible is so relevant to cattle rustlers. God says, "You shall not murder. ...You shall not covet your neighbor's...ox" (Exodus 20:13, 17). Jesus said, "love your neighbor as yourself" (Luke 19:18). This word, the word of Christ, breaks down demonic strongholds among these people, which eventually releases cultural transformation. This transformation delivers the people from poverty caused by high percentages of widows and fatherless children.

I met a tribal warrior who came to faith in a Ugandan prison. After getting out, he started evangelizing his own people. I remember him challenging an audience with his testimony. "Years ago I used to be the greatest warrior among you," he said. "I could run for miles, and I could have beaten any of you in a fight. But I met Jesus and now my life is changed! He can change your life too." The gospel catapults transformation among cultures and peoples in a way money cannot.

What Do They Have to Give?

Many who are laboring in the nations have very little to give aside from the word of Christ, especially those whom God has called from Africa. They are often not the most educated or the wealthiest. If financial lack means sleeping without a bed or a pillow, they often do it. If it means having no power or running water, they endure it. Many times, church planters from Africa, along with local believers, do not have enough money to construct a building to gather in. But they are rarely hindered by this. They gather under the shade of a tree or in a grass-thatched hut. Missionaries from Africa will travel long distances on bicycles or by foot to bring news of Jesus to those who have never heard. They may not be able to open up a food bank, give clothing, or build a hospital, and yet they can impart that which is primary. Just as Peter declared to the paralytic, "I have no silver and gold, but what I do have I give to you. In the name of Jesus Christ of Nazareth, rise up and walk" (Acts 3:6)! They declare the name of Christ and gather the flock of God to worship the Savior.

Can Africans who do not come from affluent backgrounds, who only have faith, love, and a voice, be the key to the salvation of nations? I say yes. They are entrusted with the word of Christ. In fact, many are doing far greater for the world, than even the most powerful and wealthy organizations from the West, when viewed in light of eternity. Resources are scarce and good causes abound, but consider carefully that the most important thing you might sow into is missionaries, so that they can reach the unreached with the word of Christ.

All of life is hanging on a word, therefore "receive with meekness the implanted word, which is able to save your souls" (James 1:21). And pray for the laborers in the nations, "that the word of the Lord may speed ahead and be honored" through their proclamation (2 Thessalonians 3:1).

1. DeYoung, Kevin, and Greg Gilbert. *What Is the Mission of the Church? Making Sense of Social Justice, Shalom, and the Great Commission.* Wheaton, IL: Crossway, 2011. 62.
2. Many scholars do not accept verses 9-20 as original. Many of the earliest and strongest manuscripts do not include these verses. Nevertheless, the fact that they continue to be part of our modern translation should give credence to their use. Also, the motif of preaching and casting out demons found in the gospel itself seems to in some way tie these verses to the original. Church Fathers quoted them and they are not in contradiction with other Scripture. Lastly, I am not using them to support a central doctrine, and without them the same case can still be made; for example, John 14:12 tells us that all believers can do the works that Jesus did.
3. 2 Corinthians 4:3-6
4. DeYoung, Kevin and Greg Gilbert. *What Is the Mission of the Church?* 238.
5. Yohannan, K. P. *Revolution in World Missions.* Rev. ed. Carrollton, TX: GFA Books, 2004. 111.
6. DeYoung, Kevin and Greg Gilbert. *What Is the Mission of the Church?* 246.

Above: A classroom at the School of Missions and Prayer, where African missionaries are being trained in Islamic apologetics.

Below: Jesse teaching at a "Lunch Hour Meeting" in the Uganda House of Prayer base.

Above: Students and Staff of the MAP School engaged in a Muslim-Christian debate.

Below: Student missionary reads from the Bible to a mother at the entrance to her mud house.

Above: The House of Prayer is a gathering place for the Body of Christ in the region to come together in unity to seek the Lord continually. It is the centerpiece of each missions base.

Below: The MAP School Class of 2013 graduation, including Staff families. These men and women have completed the training school and are ready to be sent to plant churches among unreached tribes.

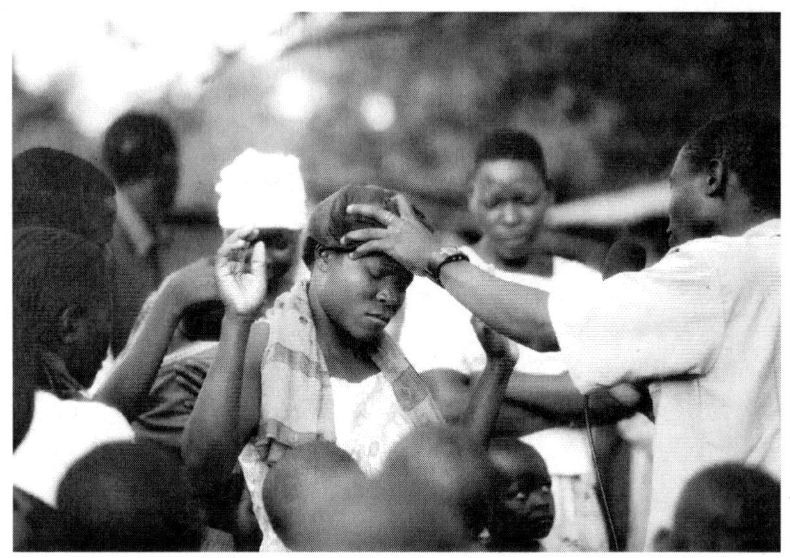

Above: A woman accepts Christ and receives prayer. Native missionaries minister the gospel with boldness, and signs and wonders follow.

Below: Student missionaries bring the truth of God's word to some of the most impoverished and outcast peoples in Africa.

Above: A new believer is baptized by Missionary Denis in a local watering hole where cattle also quench their thirst.

Below: A shepherd asks for water from our team on a desert highway in northern Kenya, and hears the name of Jesus for the first time. He received the Word with joy.

Above: Portraits of the Horn of Africa peoples during the 2011 drought and subsequent famine. Our teams were able to deliver both physical and spiritual food.

Below: Missionary William preaching the gospel to a group of Muslims in the Horn of Africa.

Above: Jesse engaged in a discussion with a Somali Muslim da'wah preacher from Nairobi on the sidelines of a public debate.

Below: Jesse sharing the gospel, at his first Muslim-Christian dialogue, to a crowd of over 1,000 Muslims in Eastern Uganda.

Above: Missionary Moses sharing the gospel with a local woman doing her laundry

Below: This old woman (right) received physical healing and rose up from her bed for the first time in months when student-missionaries (left) visited her home and prayed for her.

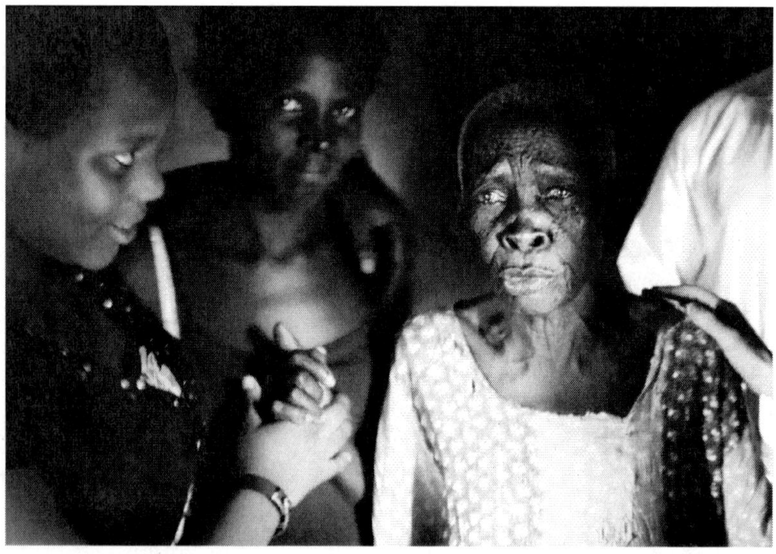

5

The Testimony of Jesus

My first organized debate was with a Somali Muslim from Nairobi. I was in my early twenties and had virtually no experience with public dialogue, and there I was standing in the center of a large field before a crowd of about a thousand Muslims. Women were sitting together, staring at me from behind their colorful hijabs, each man wearing an Islamic skullcap. I firmly made my case for the deity of Christ using traditional verses from the Gospel of John, but things were not going well, and I had a foreboding sense that I was in over my head.

We were winding down, and the crowd was in a hushed silence as a question was shot in my direction. "Give one verse in the Bible where Jesus says, 'I am God.'" I knew that there was no verse with these particular words recorded by Jesus. If he would have said it openly like this in his Jewish context, he would have been crucified on the spot! This is the reason for the round-about way he would speak of his identity. I began to answer, "There is no verse with those exact words but...." The Muslim moderator suddenly took control of the debate, and started shouting in his microphone to the audience that "the *mzungu* (white person) has admitted Jesus is not God!" As soon as the man said this, the crowd went into a frenzy with shouts of "Allahu akbar!" Then I watched as Muslims in the audience literally did summersaults right in front of our rickety wooden stage. Not the desired outcome. I tell this story because it was my baptism into the theological and spiritual war that is being waged in the nations with Islam. I was unaware and unprepared. Most people are.

The testimony of Jesus is the center of the gospel mission. The word that we spoke of in the previous chapter is the *word of Christ*. This is what it means in the book of Revelation when it tells us that the testimony of Jesus is the "Spirit of Prophecy" (Rev 19:10). All prophetic revelation and proclamation revolves around him like planets around the sun. Jesus Christ is Lord. He is the Way for all nations to know the only God. It is imperative that missionaries, and all believers, understand that their commission is to make known the lordship of Jesus in the world by the power of the Holy Spirit.

The Enemy's Primary Agenda

Satan's main agenda is to denigrate and destroy the apostolic testimony of Christ. As I continued to be involved in various dialogues in Africa, both in public venues and on the streets with everyday people, I realized just how severe the attacks against the nature of Christ are.

I once traveled in a handcrafted boat made from rough-cut timbers to an island on Lake Victoria, in Uganda. Muslim da'wah preachers were having an open-air meeting for one week, and were challenging Christian pastors on the island to a debate. As my friend and I approached the crusade along an old dirt road, we heard the speaker crying out in the Luganda language, "Anyone who says that Jesus is the Son of God is demon possessed!" He proceeded to use Matthew 16 as a proof text. Peter called Jesus the Son of God in Matthew 16:16, and just a few verses later in 16:23, Jesus rebukes him by saying "get behind me Satan!" The speaker conveniently skipped over the real reason Jesus spoke so harshly to Peter—he had denied the need for the crucifixion, which is of course what Muslims do themselves! As ridiculous as this type of argumentation is, it is having an effect where the Church is not mature or prepared. It is evident that the same enemy who was there in the wilderness while Jesus was fasting and who whispered in his ear, "if you are the son of God" is still seeking to draw multitudes away from Christ through means of deceit and twisting of Scriptures.

The great question for the world still is, "Who do people say that the Son of man is?" (Matthew 16:13). Jehovah's Witnesses answer by claiming that Jesus is the first creation of God, but not equal with Him. Mormons claim that Jesus is a god among gods. Muhammad taught that Jesus was a Muslim prophet, as were Abraham, Moses, and David. All of these diverge from the testimony of the eyewitnesses that we find in the Gospels. Islamic propagandists teach the wholesale corruption of the Gospels, and choose rather to derive their Christology from the Qur'an. The reality is that the canonical Gospels themselves are the most authoritative testimony of

Christ because they answer this question from the perspective of Jesus as shared by his closest disciples.

Bible scholar Richard Bauckam shows in his fantastic book, Jesus and the Eyewitnesses, that the Gospels are the testimony of Jesus from, well, *eyewitnesses*. As Baukham himself puts it,

> What we have in the four Gospels, in my view, is good access to *the apostolic testimony* about Jesus. *I stress the term testimony*. The eyewitnesses from whom these Gospels derive were not disinterested observers. They were involved participants in the events they later recalled and narrated. They were committed believers in the Jesus whose story they told. They and the Gospel writers were thoughtful interpreters of the significance of that story for human salvation.[1]

It is this Holy Spirit inspired testimony of Jesus which missionaries are called to proclaim as a witness to the nations.

Jesus the LORD

In Isaiah 45:21-23, YHWH (Yahweh) is proclaimed as God of the nations, and the only way of salvation.

> Was it not I, the LORD (YHWH)? And there is no other god besides me, a righteous God and a Savior; there is none besides me. Turn to me and be saved, all the ends of the earth! For I am God, and there is no other. By myself I have sworn; from my mouth has gone out in righteousness a word that shall not return: To me every knee shall bow, every tongue shall swear allegiance.

There are two primary points here. First YHWH, the God of Abraham, Isaac, and Jacob, is the only true God. He is not just a local deity among a plethora of other divine beings. He is the sovereign Lord and creator of all the earth. This echoes the Shema (the most important Jewish confession from Deuteronomy),"Hear, O Israel: The LORD our God, the LORD is one. You shall love the LORD your God with all your heart and with all your soul and with all your might" (Deuteronomy 6:4–5).

Second, the nations do not know this. They do not know the one true God who created them. So the Lord calls out to the nations to turn to him and to come under his leadership and be saved. Salvation is impossible until one comes into right relationship with the one true God, the God of Israel. But how can the nations turn to him when they don't know him, and are separated from him by sin? Paul shows us in his Christological interpretation of this passage in Philippians 2:6-11:

> Who though he was in the form of God, did not count equality with God a thing to be grasped, but made himself nothing, taking on the form of a servant, being born in the likeness of men. And being found in human form, he humbled himself by becoming obedient to the point of death, even death on a cross. Therefore God has highly exalted him and bestowed on him *the name that is above every name,* so that *at the name of Jesus every knee should bow,* in heaven and on earth and under the earth, and *every tongue confess that Jesus Christ is Lord,* to the glory of the Father. (Phil 2:6-11)

In Isaiah, YHWH says, "To me every knee will bow." Here in Philippians, it is to Jesus that "every knee should bow,...to the glory of the Father." It is through Jesus that Isaiah 45:22 will be fulfilled. Jesus is the self disclosure of God to the world, and through him the nations will be restored to relationship with the Creator.

In order to write this (and no doubt Paul understands the implication of what he is writing) he must believe that it was in fact Jesus who was speaking in Isaiah 45. Jesus is YHWH, for it was YHWH who said, "to me every knee will bow" in the context of declaring that he alone is the God of the nations. Jesus is said to have been given the name above every other name, which no doubt means that he shares the name YHWH, for it is this name alone that commands the allegiance of "every tongue"; it is the name that is above every other name. It is through Christ that eventually every nation will bow to the universal sovereignty of YHWH by confessing Jesus as Lord.

In order to guard the divine name from being taken in vain, the Greek Septuagint (the Greek translation of the Old Testament) translated YHWH with the Greek word "Kurios," which in English is "Lord." In most English Bibles, when translating the Hebrew Old Testament, "LORD" in all capital letters is used to identify where the text is showing YHWH, which is exactly what you will find in this Isaiah passage, "Was it not I, the LORD? And there is no other god besides me" (Isaiah 45:21). To call Jesus Lord (Kurios) in a context where the Greek Septuagint, known to Paul, translates the Hebrew YHWH with Kurios was provocative, especially in the Jewish scene of Paul's time. But Paul does this often in his writing, to the point where there can be no doubt of his intention to associate Jesus with YHWH.

In Romans 10, Paul tells us that salvation is a free gift that one receives by believing and confessing the Lordship of Jesus, "because, if you confess with your mouth that *Jesus is Lord* and believe in your heart that God raised him from the dead, *you will be saved*. For with the heart one believes and is justified, and with the mouth one confesses and is saved" (Romans 10:9–10). He supports his point about calling upon Jesus as Lord with a quotation from Joel 2:32, "For whoever calls upon the LORD shall be saved." Paul is not simply saying we need to believe Jesus is *a* Lord, but that he is *the* LORD.

This is not unique to Paul, but was the witness of all the apostles in the first century. James the Jewish brother of Jesus writes, "My brothers, show no partiality as you hold the faith in our Lord Jesus Christ, the Lord of glory" (James 2:1). To a Jew, there is only one Lord of glory, and that is YHWH. Yet James uses this title for Jesus in one of the earliest New Testament epistles.

So, what is the view of Jesus in the Gospels? Do the witnesses agree with Paul and James that Jesus is the LORD? The Gospel of Mark is believed by most scholars to be a work directly connected to Peter the apostle. Mark is said to have been Peter's interpreter by an early Church father named Papias. It is also held by most to be the earliest Gospel, dating within 20 to 30 years after the crucifixion.

Does Mark present Jesus as merely a prophet or as a demigod? Or does he affirm, like Paul, and James, that Jesus is the Lord of Glory? The introduction of the Gospel rules out the first two options. Right out of the gate, we have an announcement of Jesus' divine nature, "The beginning of the gospel of Jesus Christ the son of God" (Mark 1:1). This title does not have the pagan meaning of physical offspring, but rather it associates Jesus with the divine nature and makes him representative and equal to the God of Israel.

This is followed by an introduction to John the Baptist, the forerunner. John is seen as the Isaiah 40 prophet who will "prepare the way of the Lord, make his path strait" (Mark 1:3). This prophecy refers to an eschatological coming of YHWH to the earth. "The glory of the LORD shall be revealed, and all flesh shall see it together, for the mouth of the LORD has spoken" (Isaiah 40:5). The forerunner was sent to prepare for YHWH's apocalypse (revealing). In this context, it becomes plain that the one coming after John, whom John is preparing for, is Jesus; "and he preached, saying, 'After me comes he who is mightier than I, the strap of whose sandals I am not worthy to stoop down and untie'" (Mark 1:7). The Gospel of Mark uses a Hebrew prophecy about YHWH to describe the coming of Jesus.

Mark does not let up at this point, but drives home the comparison, recording John the Baptist's words "I have baptized you with water, but he will baptize you with the Holy Spirit" (Mark 1:8). This verse has deep Christological inference, for it is only YHWH who may administrate the Holy Spirit; "And I will put my Spirit within you, and cause you to walk in my statutes and be careful to obey my rules" (Ezekiel 36:27). "And it shall come to pass afterward, that I will pour out my Spirit on all flesh" (Joel 2:28). There should be no doubt of Mark's intention to present Jesus in this Gospel as YHWH, the God of Israel, come in the flesh.

It is through the testimony of Jesus that the nations will come to know the one true God of Israel; he is the Lord. It is the responsibility of missionaries to proclaim his name and his testimony in the earth. More and more, this message will be challenged and resisted, sometimes with violence. It is not our talk about Jesus that makes the world angry, but our talk that he is Lord. It is the Lord Jesus that so many in the nations resist and that devils try to impugn. It is imperative upon this generation of believers and missionaries to know their Lord. And it is our mission to proclaim him with boldness.

Boldness

When Paul thinks about his missionary task in preaching Christ to the nations, he asks the Church, "At the same time, pray also for us, that God may open to us a door for the word, to declare the mystery of Christ, on account of which I am in prison—that I may make it clear, which is how I ought to speak" (Colossians 4:3–4). There is a way that one ought to speak about Christ; with clarity and not timidity. It is essential for believers to guard and fight against the fear of man, "for God has not given us a spirit of fear but of power and love and self-control. Therefore do not be ashamed of the testimony about our Lord, nor of me his prisoner, but share in suffering for the gospel by the power of God" (2 Timothy 1:7-8). The Bible promises that the Holy Spirit will give us boldness to speak. Boldness is the ability to bear witness about the Lord Jesus in the midst of adversity.

I believe there is a great need for Holy Spirit boldness on the mission field today. Boldness is not usually included in missional strategy. Instead many opt for safe models of evangelism that do not require risk. This is especially true in Muslim evangelism. We will never reach the Muslim world for Christ by hiding his true identity or simply by making friendships with Muslims. We must boldly proclaim the lordship of Jesus to Muslims around the world. We do it in a spirit of gentleness, but without shame or fear.

I have never felt more acutely aware of the need for boldness than when we launched a church plant among the Banuin[2] tribe. Our team of second-year student missionaries engaged this Muslim community in evangelism and outreach. It was amazing to see this small tribe, almost completely insulated from outsiders and from Christian witness, in the middle of a country where Christians are the majority. They migrated to the area over a century ago and acquired land that they maintain as strictly Islamic territory.

One evening, we decided to reach the main trading center where these people gather. The goal was to show the Jesus Film, something we had done in other Islamic areas with great success. This night would be different. We found a densely populated area and started setting up the equipment. When people began to notice what was going on, they came over to observe us with great suspicion. We told them we wanted to show a movie about Isa (Jesus) and the Injil (gospel), but when they realized we were Christians, they immediately became aggressive: "This place is for Muslims. We don't want Christians here!" Within minutes, we were being surrounded by an angry mob, so we rushed to pack up our equipment and leave. The threats starting picking up. "You have three minutes before we light your van on fire!" The team quickly got in the vehicle as we started driving away, with equipment still on the roof. The crowds began hitting the sides and back of the car and yelling that we should never return, "Allahu Akbar!" This is the way that the Banuins (and many other Islamic tribes) have remained unreached for generations; they fight to protect their culture and religion.

So what do you do when you get chased out of town? We decided to preach in the next trading center a mile down the road. Here, we were able to show the film and pray for the sick. The next night we held our first open-air evangelistic meeting and proclaimed the gospel of Jesus. The following night, the mob struck again. A group of about forty people led by a local Imam came shouting and heckling us to stop the event immediately. Local police had caught wind of the plan to attack us and armed officers appeared, commanding us to stop the event until we could sort out the problem. We conceded as the crowd continued to grow and get louder, shouting that if we ever preached again, they would kill us and burn down the Christian shop owner's building where we had staged the meeting.

The next day, the Imam stood by the roadside at his car, waiting to see if we were going to try preaching again. I approached him and offered my hand in greeting, but before I could even say hello the threats rolled in. He lifted finger to throat and slid it left to right. "If you preach here again, know that we are ready to shed blood and die for Allah!"

I said the first thing that came to mind. "We are ready to die for Jesus, but are not here to fight." Then I questioned him about the meaning of Islam. "Doesn't Islam mean peace? Why are you are threatening us when we haven't spoken anything evil against your religion?"

He paused for a moment, then promised, "Islam is a religion of peace. As long as you stay in the church and don't preach publicly, and don't try to interpret the Qur'an, then we will leave you alone." Such is the nature of Islam's doctrine of peace. With public meetings shut down by intimidated local government officials, we decided to hit the streets and continued with door-to-door outreach.

The team spent one week with the Banuins and received multiple threats. They were chased from homes and towns with words and weapons. In the midst of it, God was moving and touching hearts. There were Muslims that night defending us against the crowd, saying that our message was good and they wanted to hear more. An elderly woman was healed when two members of the team prayed for her damaged ankle. She invited them to come to her home and share Christ. Unfortunately, her children caught wind of it and chased the evangelists from the house with a machete! In spite of the obstacles, God seemed to have opened the heavens and the hearts of many who had no one to tell them the gospel. The irrationality of those who attacked us, having failed to refute our teaching, was put on display. So was the love of Christ. Like a dam being broken so that water can flow, our preaching and outreach in the area was breaking open new doors in the region, preparing the way for others who would remain as full-time missionaries.

This mission was a test for the whole team and the local believers we were working with. Would we fear and hide our witness? Would we rise up in pride and anger against the Banuin Muslims because of how they treated the believers? We spent a lot of time crying out to the Lord for wisdom, love, and boldness. Wisdom to know when to speak and when to be silent. Love for the Banuin people, especially the ones who were persecuting and threatening us. Boldness not to be silent, even at the cost of our lives.

Two *Send56* missionaries remained in the area and continued to reach out to the Banuin people, when suddenly God opened a way for the gospel. The Islamic community put on a one week open-air da'wah event, where they openly refute Christianity and preach about Islam. The missionaries were ready, trained in the Qur'an and how to answer Islam. Each day, for five days, they were given opportunity to speak, and they openly testified about Christ amidst the ridicule of the community and organizers. On the last day I joined the fray, and they allowed me to debate on the crucifixion of Jesus. There before a crowd of unreached Muslims, in the very place where they had chased us away one year previous, the gospel of salvation and the atonement of Jesus was being proclaimed. The audience was struck that Christians had knowledge of the Qur'an, and were challenging the assertions of the sheikhs. Since that time, through the labors of the African missionaries, eight Banuins have come to know Christ and a church is being planted among them. Banuins were 0.00% Christian, but new doors are opening for the gospel.

Boldness in the Early Church

When the Holy Spirit is poured out in Acts 2, tongues of fire rest on the heads of the disciples as they begin to speak in other tongues. I believe this symbol represents the word of the Lord. Jeremiah says about the prophetic witness, "Let the prophet who has a dream tell the dream, but let him who has my word speak my word faithfully....Is not my word like fire, declares the LORD, and like a hammer that breaks the rock in pieces" (Jeremiah 23:28-29). The fire is the power of prophetic witness. This is confirmed by how the fire appears as a tongue and is linked with the gift of tongues, which is supernatural utterance. The people "hear them telling in our own tongues the mighty works of God" (Acts 2:11). When Peter begins to explain the phenomenon that is occurring to the astounded observers, he explains that this is the fulfillment of Joel 2:32. There, the outpouring of the Holy Spirit will directly translate into prophetic proclamation by sons, daughters, male servants, and female servants, "I will pour out my Spirit on all flesh, and your sons and your daughters shall prophesy… even on my male servants and female servants in those days I will pour out my Spirit, and they shall prophesy" (Acts 2:17-18). The result of the outpouring of the Holy Spirit in the life of the early Church is astounding.

At the end of Peter's proclamation, he directly confronts the very people who crucified Christ, telling them without fear, "Let all the house of Israel therefore know for certain that God has made him both Lord and Christ, This Jesus whom you crucified" (Acts 2:36). This man, who had recently denied Christ in the very same city because he feared for his life, was now walking in supernatural boldness and "when they heard this they were cut to the heart, and said to Peter and the rest of the apostles, 'Brothers, what shall we do?'" (Acts 2:37). He tells them to, "Repent and be baptized every one of you in the name of Jesus Christ for the forgiveness of your sins, and you will receive the gift of the Holy Spirit....And with many other words he bore witness and continued to exhort them, saying, 'save yourselves from this crooked generation'" (Acts 2:40). That is boldness.

It is no surprise that the same religious leaders who had Jesus put to death would soon become enraged that the Jesus movement was not exactly withering after the crucifixion, "And as they were speaking to the people, the priests and the captain of the temple and the Sadducees came upon them, greatly annoyed because they were teaching the people and proclaiming in Jesus the resurrection from the dead and they arrested them..." (Acts 4:1-3). After the arrest, they begin to question Peter and John, "By what power or by what name did you do this" (Acts 4:7)? The Holy Spirit releases boldness to confront rulers with the gospel of Christ, "Then Peter filled with the Holy Spirit, said to them,...there is salvation in no one else, for there is no other name under heaven given among men by which we must be saved'" (Acts 4:8, 12).

At this point in 4:13, the text notes that the religious leaders, "saw the boldness of Peter and John, and perceived that they were uneducated, common men, they were astonished. And they recognized that they had been with Jesus." It is clear that the Holy Spirit is the power behind their witness, and from an outside perspective the Sadducees translate Holy Spirit boldness as evidence of the apostles' relationship with Jesus. The Holy Spirit empowers the witness of Christ. Finally, the rulers charge them, "...not to speak or teach at all in the name of Jesus" (Acts 4:18). The apostles know that is not an option, "whether it is right in the sight of God to listen to you rather than to God, you must judge, for we cannot but speak of what we have seen and heard" (Acts 4:19-20).

This encounter brings the Church to a decisive point in their early existence; do we quiet down or keep proclaiming Jesus and the resurrection? So they gather and cry out to God, "And now, Lord, look upon their threats and grant to your servants to continue to speak your word with all boldness" (Acts 4:29). That day, another mighty outpouring of the Holy Spirit falls on the Church in Jerusalem. The Bible says, "they were all filled with the Holy Spirit and continued to speak the word of God with boldness" (Acts 4:31).

This kind of Holy Spirit boldness, is what I have witnessed coming from African believers. God is enlisting thousands of men and women who are unafraid to cry out and declare that Jesus is Lord. I once went on a trip to the northern part of Uganda which required traveling on two different buses. On the first bus, I sat down and the young fiery believer we were traveling with stood up and started sharing the gospel with everyone on the bus. He marched up and down the center aisle, swaying back and forth while the driver dodged potholes. He managed to share Christ with everyone on the bus and then pray for those who wanted to receive the message.

I thought this was exciting, but that was only the start. He sat down and the driver stopped to pick up more passengers. Another young preacher came onto the bus and declared the gospel in his native Luganda tongue and then got off before the bus continued on the road. I was stunned! It is not every day you see someone willing to publicly share the gospel, and certainly not common to see two unconnected people do it on the same bus. But this is common in Uganda, which is full of preachers who seem literally to be crying out on every street corner. What is the role of the African preacher in this generation? Could it be that God has called such a remarkable generation, poor economically, but rich in faith, to help finish the Great Commission and bring in an end time harvest in the Islamic world?

An African pastor once told me the key to breakthrough in his Muslim-majority area. He said that he was willing to interact with the Muslim apologists in public debate. For one month, everyday, he engaged in public dialogues with the local Islamic community. Although these could be quite controversial, the atmosphere began to change, and Muslims who were hostile and unwilling to talk to Christians, would now engage in more conversations. Seeing that a Christian could interact with the Qur'an and argue from Scriptures actually made them more receptive to the gospel, or at least respectful toward this Christian pastor. After thirty days, Muslims began to come to his church and he saw weekly conversions.

Depending on the area and sensitivity of the Muslim population, this may or may not be possible. Anyone sharing the gospel in a Muslim area needs to be aware of what the Muslims believe, and be culturally sensitive to those beliefs. Nevertheless, any evangelism in the Islamic context that does not include a clear presentation of Christ as Lord, and a real call to renounce Islamic false doctrines, is not the right method.

A Threefold Victory Plan

The book of Revelation gives us a threefold victory plan for the end of the age, and the testimony of Jesus is right in the center of it. The strategy is purity, testimony, and martyrdom: "And they have conquered him by *the blood of the Lamb* and by the *word of their testimony,* for they loved not their lives *even unto death*" (Revelation 12:11).

Purity

Purity comes from the blood of the Lamb, "these are the ones coming out of the great tribulation. They have washed their robes and made them white in the blood of the Lamb" (Revelation 7:14). The paradoxical expression here is to show the powerful work of the blood of Christ. Red makes white. The blood of Christ is the agent that cleanses sin, "and from Jesus Christ the faithful witness, the first born from the dead, and the ruler of the kings of the earth. To him who loved us and has freed us from our sins by his blood" (Revelation 1:5). The blood of Christ worked to justify us and works to sanctify us.

We also have an active part to play in washing our robes, so that they can be clean on the Day of Judgment. John says it like this, "and everyone who thus hopes in him purifies himself as he is pure" (1 John 3:4). When we walk in fellowship, confess sin, and live in transparency, it unleashes the power of grace in our life for holiness: "But if we walk in the light, as he is in the light, we have fellowship with one another, and the blood of Jesus his Son cleanses us from all sin....If we confess our sins, he is faithful and just to forgive us our sins and to cleanse us from all unrighteousness" (1 John 1:7–9).

Living a pure life is an essential part of spiritual warfare. John says "We know that everyone who has been born of God does not keep on sinning, but he who was born of God protects him, and the evil one does not touch him" (1 John 5:18). Paul warns us about a time of intensified spiritual warfare, and tells us the first line of defense against the enemy is moral righteousness, "Therefore take up the whole armor of God, that you may be able to withstand in the evil day....having fastened the belt of truth, and having put on the breastplate of righteousness." Purity is crucial to the victory.

Testimony

Next and center is "the word of their testimony." At a glance, one may think that this means their individual salvation stories. That is not the case here. Just a few verses later, we find out more specifically what the testimony is, "Then the dragon became furious with the woman and went off to make war on the rest of her offspring, on those who keep the commandments of God and hold the testimony of

Jesus" (Revelation 12:17). The victory of the saints is in the testimony of Jesus.

We can also see this in chapter 1. The author identifies himself as John, a servant of Christ, "who bore witness to the word of God and to the testimony of Jesus Christ" (Revelation 1:2). So the word of John's testimony is Christ. He also says that it was because of the "testimony of Jesus" that he is a "brother and partner in the tribulation" of the saints (Revelation 1:9). In the same way, the martyrs of Revelation 6:9 suffer because of their witness, "When he opened the fifth seal, I saw under the altar the souls of those who had been slain for the word of God and for the witness they had borne." Undoubtedly, their testimony was the same as John's —they bore witness of Christ, and for that witness were killed.

All believers will win this way. All saints must speak, and all saints must pray for boldness to testify about Jesus. This is why Paul gives thanks for God's work among the Corinthian believers, "that in every way you were enriched in him in all speech and all knowledge—even as the testimony about Christ was confirmed among you" (1 Corinthians 1:4-6). The testimony of Christ was being confirmed among them as they were operating in the word of knowledge. They were speaking to one another about who God is in Christ. This was their testimony. Another time, he tells the Church in Colossae to, "let the word of Christ dwell in you richly, teaching and admonishing one another in all wisdom, singing psalms and hymns and spiritual songs, with thankfulness in your hearts toward God" (Col 3:16). This is how the Church succeeds, by making Christ all in all in our fellowship and speech.

This anointed word of Christ declared by his people to each other and to all nations is the spirit of prophecy. After an encounter with an angel, John is overcome. He says, "Then I fell down at his feet to worship him, but he said to me, 'You must not do that! I am a fellow servant with you and your brothers who hold to the testimony of Jesus. Worship God.' For the testimony of Jesus is the spirit of prophecy" (Revelation 19:10). I believe this is exactly what Joel 2 was talking about. In the last days, the Holy Spirit will be poured out on all nations, and the children of God everywhere will prophecy; they will bear witness of Christ, the Word made flesh. The nations will glorify the one God by turning to Jesus through *the word of their testimony*.

Martyrdom

The final part of the strategy is martyrdom. Because of the testimony of Jesus, the devil will hate believers and even kill some of them and put them is prison. He hated Christ and killed him. Jesus warned us that, "you will be hated by all for my name's sake. But the one who endures to the end will be saved" (Mark. 13:13). He also said,

> If the world hates you, know that it has hated me before it hated you. If you were of the world, the world would love you as its own; but because you are not of the world, but I chose you out of the world, therefore the world hates you. Remember the word that I said to you: 'A servant is not greater than his master.' If they persecuted me, they will also persecute you. If they kept my word, they will also keep yours. But all these things they will do to you on account of my name, because they do not know him who sent me. (John 15:18-21)

It is on account of his name that Christians will be hated—because of the testimony we hold.

Yet, it is in the valuing of the witness of Christ over our temporal life that we will conquer Satan, for, "they did not love their lives even unto death." This part of the victory is precisely because the testimony of Jesus is a witness of resurrection. Death has no power over the saints. For a believer, dying for the name of Christ is the crown of witness.

In chapter 13 of Revelation, the end-time beast empire comes into authority over the whole earth and amazingly, "it was allowed to make war on the saints and to conquer them" (Revelation 13:7). So who conquers...the beast or the saints? The answer is that the beast's victory is temporal but the saint's victory is eternal. The saint's victory is by resurrection from the dead, thereby giving credence to the creed they confess! Jesus is Lord, his death overcame sin, and his power overcame death. This is a victory of faith.

The devil hates the children of God so much, he will make the same mistake with us that he made with Jesus; he will try to eradicate and destroy us. But that will only seal his fate, because it will confirm our testimony. In this way, dying and suffering for Christ is martyrdom, which is the word for *witness* in the Greek. It was through death that Christ conquered death and the devil, and, "none of the rulers of this age understood this, for if they had, they would not have crucified the Lord of Glory" (1 Corinthians 2:9). This is laid out in Romans:

> What shall we say to these things? If God is for us, who can be against us?....Who shall bring a charge against God's elect? It is God who justifies. Who is to condemn? Christ Jesus is the one who died—more

> than that, who was raised—who is at the right hand of God....who shall separate us from the love of Christ? Shall tribulation, or distress, or persecution, or famine, or nakedness, or danger, or sword? As it is written, 'For your sake we are being killed all day long; we are regarded as sheep to be slaughtered' No, in all these things *we are more than conquerors* through him who loved us. For I am sure that neither death nor life...will be able to separate us from the love of God in Christ Jesus our Lord. (Romans 8:31-39)

We are conquerors, even in and through death, for the love of God is stronger than the grave. In Revelation 20:4, we see those who were killed as those who have victory and reign with Christ:

> Then I saw thrones, and seated on them were those to whom the authority to judge was committed. Also I saw the souls of *those who had been beheaded for the testimony of Jesus and for the word of God,* and those who had not worshiped the beast or its image and had not received its mark on their foreheads or their hands. *They came to life and reigned* with Christ for a thousand years.

We Must Know Christ

What does this all mean for missions to the unreached? It means we must know Christ. You cannot proclaim who you do not know. I am deeply concerned that there should be more awareness related to the theological and missiological challenge facing the Church with Islam. Many are not prepared, and their faith will be shaken if they are not deeply rooted in their relationship with Jesus. Paul prays that we would know Christ more: "that the God of our Lord Jesus Christ, the Father of glory, may give you the Spirit of wisdom and of revelation in the knowledge of him" (Ephesians 1:17).

I can identify two ways that we should come to know Jesus more from his own words:

> On the last day of the feast, the great day, Jesus stood up and cried out, "If anyone thirsts, let him come to me and drink. Whoever believes in me, as the Scripture has said, 'Out of his heart will flow rivers of living water.'" Now this he said about the Spirit, whom those who believed in him were to receive, for as yet the Spirit had not been given, because Jesus was not yet glorified. (John 7:37–39)

First is the need to study and know the Scriptures. Nothing can replace personal time with Jesus in his word. Notice that he tells us that the Scriptures speak of him. He is referring to the Torah, the Psalms, and the Prophets in the Old Testament. All these testify of him, and if we want to know him then we must know them. We are not to believe in any Jesus, but the Jesus of the Scriptures. We believe in him on his terms.

Second, we come to know him more through the Holy Spirit, who Jesus promised would flow from our hearts "like rivers of living water." By the Spirit, in prayer, we gaze upon the beauty of Jesus: "And we all, with unveiled face, beholding the glory of the Lord, are being transformed into the same image from one degree of glory to another. For this comes from the Lord who is the Spirit" (2 Corinthians 3:17–

18). Through prayer we come to know the Lord intimately. This intimacy leads to confidence and boldness in the face of all obstacles. As Paul said, "I am not ashamed, for I know whom I have believed, and I am convinced that he is able to guard until that Day what has been entrusted to me" (2 Timothy 1:12).

What a great need there is today for those who say, "But whatever gain I had, I counted as loss for the sake of Christ. Indeed, I count everything as loss because of the surpassing worth of knowing Christ Jesus my Lord" (Philippians 3:7–8). This is how Paul could say "For to me to live is Christ, and to die is gain" (Philippians 1:21). Let us pray together for a generation of believers who know Christ deeply, and are not afraid to proclaim the way of salvation for all people: Jesus the Lord of glory.

1. Bauckham, Richard. *Jesus and the Eyewitnesses: The Gospels as Eyewitness Testimony*. Grand Rapids, Mich.: William B. Eerdmans Pub, 2006. 9.
2. For security reasons the name of this tribe has been changed.

6

Unceasing Prayer for the Harvest

The Great Commission will be accomplished the same place it began—in the prayer room. This is indicated by the instructions Jesus gave the disciples when he observed the need for laborers in the harvest. He does not make an appeal for more workers, he makes an appeal for more prayer: "Then he said to his disciples, 'The harvest is plentiful, but the laborers are few; therefore pray earnestly to the Lord of the harvest to send out laborers into his harvest'" (Matthew 9:37-38).

It is radical to risk the entire enterprise on prayer, but this is what Jesus does. No prayer, no harvest. Delegating the success of the mission to prayer means that it is delegated to God. The mission is absolutely and utterly dependent upon God's sovereign power, which he chooses to implement with the participation of his saints.

Our Access to the Risen Lord

Prayer is our connection to Christ who is alive in heaven. The resurrection of Jesus Christ caused an explosive expansion in the first century Church living in a Jewish world. These early Jewish monotheists experienced something that made them worshippers of a Rabbi, and followers of a faith they were willing to die just to speak about. According to the apostolic testimony, they saw that Rabbi crucified, buried, and miraculously alive again! They claimed to watch him ascend into heaven with a physical body. He himself had predicted that he would rise from the dead, and this was the proof of his authority and of his claim to divinity.

If the resurrection is the *explanation* for the explosion and expansion of the early Church, then prayer was the *fuel* behind it. The continuing impact of the resurrection, through the witness of the apostles, was brought about by a community still very much connected to the risen Lord, through the Spirit, by prayer. It was through prayer that they not only became witnesses of the resurrection, but also participants in his life and conduits of his power. Prayer was real-time access to the One who had risen, and who sent the Spirit to confirm the heavenly reality.

Jesus told the disciples just before he went to the cross that they would remain connected to him through prayer, even though he had gone to heaven: "Truly, truly, I say to you, whoever believes in me will also do the works that I do; and greater works than these will he do, because I am going to the Father. Whatever you ask in my name, this I will do, that the Father may be glorified in the Son. If you ask me anything in my name, I will do it" (John 14:12-14). Believers will do more than he did because he now represents them from a heavenly position. When the disciples ask him from earth, he will answer them from heaven. Jesus himself will act on their behalf. He would do this by sending them another Helper, the Holy Spirit, to abide with them and communicate his heart to them: "And I will ask the Father, and he will give you another Helper, to be with you forever" (John 14:16).

The Holy Spirit uniquely helps the saints to abide in Christ, to know his will and hear his words, though he does not live in the world. We are still connected to him; he is in us and we are in him, by the Spirit:

> Nevertheless, I tell you the truth: it is to your advantage that I go away, for if I do not go away, the Helper will not come to you. But if I go, I will send him to you. (John 16:7)
>
> He will glorify me, for he will take what is mine and declare it to you. All that the Father has is mine; therefore I said that he will take what is mine and declare it to you. (John 16:14-15)

After the resurrection, Jesus' instructions to the community of believers was to "tarry in Jerusalem" until they received the promise of the Holy Spirit. So they went into the upper room and devoted themselves to prayer. The early Church was birthed in a prayer room:

> They went up to the upper room, where they were staying, Peter and John and James and Andrew, Philip and Thomas, Bartholomew and Matthew, James the son of Alphaeus and Simon the Zealot and Judas the son of James. All these with one accord were devoting

> themselves to prayer, together with the women and Mary the mother of Jesus, and his brothers. (Acts 1:13-14)

On the day of Pentecost, Jesus did what he promised and sent the Holy Spirit, who was poured out on the praying saints. Amazingly, after the wind and the fire, after the 3,000 were saved in Jerusalem, after they received what was spoken by the prophet Joel, they proceeded with their devotion and corporate prayer life. They didn't stop praying once the Holy Spirit was poured out. They only prayed with more zeal. The move of the Spirit in Acts 2 was not the end, as if they would only be filled once. The Holy Spirit filled the believers again and gave them greater faith and power as they continued devoting themselves to prayer. They continued accessing the divine life of Christ by maintaining their devotion.

> And they devoted themselves to the apostles' teaching and the fellowship, to the breaking of bread and the prayers. (Acts 2:42)
>
> And when they had prayed, the place in which they were gathered together was shaken, and they were all filled with the Holy Spirit and continued to speak the word of God with boldness. (Acts 4:31)

The early Church's devotional, almost monastic commitment to prayer can also be seen in the Apostles themselves, who saw prayer as their fundamental ministry, "But we will devote ourselves to prayer and to the ministry of the word" (Acts 6:4).

This commitment is also apparent with the widows mentioned in 1 Timothy 5, who were taken care of by the

Church and expected to give themselves to a life of prayer: "She who is truly a widow, left all alone, has set her hope on God and continues in supplications and prayers night and day....Let a widow be enrolled if she is not less than sixty years of age, having been the wife of one husband" (1 Tim 5:5,9).

An Eternal Calling

Prayer was at the center of the early Church's missional community, because it is the core of the Church's eternal identity and destiny. We were created for communion with God, and prayer is the mechanism of that communion. Prayer cannot therefore be just another aspect of our Christianity, but needs to be the center of it. The saints must be devoted to prayer, as they were in the early Church. Prayer shouldn't be part of the program, it should *be* the program.

Prayer is our eternal calling from God. God has always existed in divine fellowship; Father, Son, and Holy Spirit. God is *persons,* and that is why human beings are persons with form, emotion, and the need for community. We pray because God prays. Usually prayer is equated only with petition, and while it is true that petition is part of prayer, prayer is first about communion. Communion and petition begin with and spring forth from God. We see this in Genesis 1:26 when God says, "let us make man in our image." "Let us" is a clear indication of plurality, that God is requesting participation from God in the divine purpose of creating man in his own image. God is speaking to God in order to actualize his eternal will. Man was not created in the image of angels or any other creature, and the fact that there is plurality in God is not only suggested with the use of "Us" in God's reference to himself, but also in the very creation of mankind as man and woman: "So God created man in his own image…male and female he created them" (Genesis 1:27). This "one flesh" unity of persons reflects the divine persons of the Godhead, a plurality in unity.

This communion of the Godhead is nowhere more clearly reflected than in the astounding prayer of Jesus in John 17:1-26. Jesus the Son is praying to the Father. The Son is pre-existent according to verse 5, "And now, Father, glorify me in your own presence with the glory that I had with you before the world existed," and in verse 24, "you loved me before the foundation of the world." When we overhear the Son speaking in earnest with his Father, we are listening to the continuation of an eternal dialogue, one that harkens back to Genesis 1:26.

This prayer of Jesus brings us deep into the plan of God's heart, showing that God is uniting his people to himself, involving them in the shared life of the Trinity forever. There are several ways that God has invited his people into the Trinitarian fellowship.

First, in the experience of love, "that the world may know that you...loved them even as you loved me" (John 17:23). God loves us the same way he loves himself, and he revealed this through Christ.

Second, in the unity and spiritual relationship existing in God. The statement "I in them and you in me" (John 17:23) shows that we are being brought into the very life and fellowship of the Trinity.

Third, we are given access to behold and worship the beauty and glory of Christ forever, "That they also, whom you have given me, may be with me where I am, to see my glory" (John 17:24). This is the most wonderful thing that God could give to any creature, for to see him is to be filled with joy unspeakable and never-ending. The very desire of the Son that we would be near him and behold his glory is also the thing that will eternally satisfy the heart of the Bride.

Lastly, we share in the divine fellowship through *prayer.* This means that we also get to be part of the conversation that the Father and the Son have been having from before time. Imagine walking into a room occupied by heads-of-state, engaged in deep dialogue. Then, not only do they invite you to sit in their circle, but they look at you and want you to get involved in their talk! The Father, Son, and Holy Spirit, who exist in divine and eternal fellowship, creating and running the universe, have invited you into their circle; they want to hear your voice and they want you to speak and ask for things that will bring forth the divine purpose.

Since prayer begins within God, we should not imagine that prayer is temporal or simply supplication. Prayer is eternal. It is the relational mechanism between God and God, and therefore between man and God. It is the mechanism of communion and the calling of every disciple. That is why it is the eternal calling of the Church. The Lord said, "my house shall be called a house of prayer for all peoples" (Isaiah. 56:7). In the heavenly realm, the prayer meeting never ends. There is unceasing worship around the throne of God (Revelation 4-5).

In this eternal and divine relationship with God through prayer, the saints participate in his purpose. Purpose presupposed with words like "Father I desire" (John 17:24). God has massive desires, and therefore he has a massive purpose. The Father commands the Son, "Ask of me, and I will make the nations your heritage, and the ends of the earth your possession" (Psalm 2:8). What purpose! Jesus ever lives to make intercession for this end, and bids his saints, "Pray the Lord of the harvest." The praying Church is the Church on mission with God.

The Moravians: Prayer, Awakening, Missions

There is probably no better example of a praying church giving rise to missions than that of the Moravians. On August 13, 1727, there was an outpouring of the Spirit that completely transformed a new and diverse community in Saxony, Germany, a community that had come to live as refugees on the estate of Count Nicolaus Ludwig Von Zinzendorf. That day is remembered as the "Moravian Pentecost." Two weeks later, forty families from the group decided to begin an hourly intercession, praying round the clock, twenty-four hours a day. They were sentries standing before the Lord, for his purpose in their community and in the nations. More people joined over time, and for more than one hundred years without stopping, the community at Herrnhut kept the "Lord's Watch" day and night. Herrnhut seems to be an almost unmentioned catalyst of the first Great Awakening. It became a center of a spiritual renewal itself, and was visited by men like John Wesley, who said of it:

> I would gladly have spent my life here; but my Master was calling me to labor in another part of his vineyard, I was constrained to take my leave of this happy place....O when shall THIS Christianity cover the earth, as the "waters cover the sea?"[1]

Moravian brother Peter Bolher led John Wesley to a saving relationship with Christ while he was in Georgia.

John's brother Charles, one of the greatest hymn writers in history, remained connected to the Moravians until the end of his life. My speculation is that beyond the influence they had on men like John and Charles Wesley, the Moravians' impact in the Great Awakening was greatest through the never-ending prayer chain going on in Herrnhut. Could it be that their intercession was fueling the explosive power of God's Spirit that was sweeping across Europe and America and spreading to the nations? But we need not stay in speculation to feel the weight of what God did with these praying saints from Herrnhut.

Night and day prayer gave birth to missions. Zinzendorf was gripped with a zeal for the nations. "God has given me, be he thanked, a tireless spirit to further his honor and fame, a spirit that can never rest."[2] And the cry of Wesley, "when shall THIS Christianity cover the earth," was already the burden of so many of the Moravians themselves. God was giving them dreams and visions of bringing the gospel to foreign lands. Missionaries from Germany would visit the American Indians a decade before Brainerd. Soon after the prayer watch began, missionaries started to go—to slaves in the Caribbean, Eskimos in Greenland, to South America, and to the southern tip of Africa. Still more went to the American Indians, then to the Gold Coast of Africa, Algeria, Egypt, Persia, and India. Within Zinzendorf's lifetime, hundreds would be sent and eventually thousands would travel to distant lands with the gospel of Christ. This was in a time when sending missionaries to unreached peoples was almost unheard of. William Carey, considered the founder of modern missions, fed up with the lack of zeal for the nations among his denomination, appealed to the example of the Moravians: "See what the Moravians have done! Cannot we follow their example and in obedience to our Heavenly Master go out into the world, and preach the Gospel to the heathen?"[3]

Missionaries traveling out of the prayer chamber had a powerful and lasting impact wherever they went. These were men and women of total devotion. They practiced a radical obedience to the leadership of the Holy Spirit, and a willingness to go wherever he sent them. They spoke about exuberant joy in Christ and the "religion of the heart." They saw slaves as their equals, learned indigenous languages, and were not afraid to die for the sake of the gospel. Zinzendorf himself declared "I have been commissioned by the Lord God to spread the word of Jesus' blood, without concern as to what happens to me as a result."[4] They had one passion—Christ. Hutton writes, "When the Brethren went out to preach, they made His Sacrificial Death, His Holy Life, and His abiding presence the main substance of their Gospel message."[5]

The Moravians prove that prayer can be at the center of the local Church's communal expression. And I believe further than that, they show that prayer *should* be at the center. For if the Church makes prayer the center of practice, the result will be the nations coming to know Christ. Prayer will always lead to and empower missions.

Is this not what the Scriptures teach? Paul writes, "do not be anxious about anything, but in everything by prayer and supplication with thanksgiving let your requests be made known to God" (Philippians 4:6). What a stunning phrase —"In everything by prayer." If this is true, our whole life should be saturated with prayer. Life in Christ is a life of prayer. E. M. Bounds was right, "when faith ceases to pray, it ceases to live."[6] Paul tells the Thessalonian believers to "Pray without ceasing" (Thessalonians 5:17), and the Ephesian believers to pray "at all times in the Spirit, with all prayer and supplication. To that end keep alert with all perseverance, making supplication for all the saints" (Ephesians 6:18). If there is one thing the Church must do all the time, it is to pray. The Moravians took this very seriously. They did not minimize the command, they obeyed it. Zinzendorf had a conviction that revival must be sustained by abiding prayer in the life of the community. He believed that the prayers of the saints were like incense that should rise to God continually. What came forth as a result of that incense in Saxony shifted the entire course of history.

Prayer and Discipleship

Disciples of Christ, effective in the world, are forged in Christian communities, committed to continual prayer. Otherwise, as E. M. Bounds so aptly warns us, there will not be success:

> Failure has resulted from a lack of trust, or from a weakness of faith, and this, in turn, from a lack of prayerfulness. Many a failure in revival efforts has been traceable to the same cause. Faith had not been nurtured and made powerful by prayer. Neglect of the inner chamber is the solution of most spiritual failure.[7]

It is critical that the people of God learn to pray. Missionaries must learn how to pour out their soul in prayer before they will be fit to pour out their life for the world. They must learn to wrestle with God in supplications before they can fight with principalities in the nations. Without prayer, they cannot learn the lesson that nothing is actually accomplished *for* God, but rather everything is done *through* God by prayer. Missionaries must be forged with the fire of the Holy Spirit, on the anvil of a prayerful life, with the hammer of the word of God. They must be sent forth from the prayer room.

David Brainerd

If anyone can show us the truth in this, it is David Brainerd. In the 1740s, he gave his twenties to bring the gospel to the Native Indians in the Northeast American colonies. He did this while struggling with chronic sickness and fatigue, until he died in the home of Jonathan Edwards (famous theologian, pastor, and missionary during the Great Awakening) on October 9, 1747, at the young age of 29.

Even before what he would consider his actual conversion, when he came to a saving faith in Christ and a true repentance from sin, he was hungry for God. "Sometime in February, 1739, I set apart a day for secret fasting and prayer and spent the day in almost incessant cries to God for mercy,"[8] Brainerd writes. He continued seeking until July 12, 1739, when he describes a moment where God reveals himself in a unique way to him. "My soul was so captivated and delighted with the excellency, loveliness, greatness, and other perfections of God that I was even swallowed up in him,"[9] he writes. After an unfortunate misunderstanding and expulsion from Yale University, he began to pursue missionary endeavors.

It is his love for the presence of God and his continual pursuit of holiness that strikes me as I read his diary. He had uncommon and single-hearted devotion to the presence of God in prayer. He traveled and preached in various areas of

New Jersey, New York, Delaware, Connecticut, and New England, all the while enduring loneliness, frequent depression, and chronic illness. Yet through all this, he conquered by an unyielding prayer life. He frequently spoke of entering agonizing intercession. "The Lord visited me marvelously in prayer," he says:

> I think my soul never was in such agony before. I felt no restraint; for the treasures of divine grace were open to me. I wrestled for absent friends, for the ingathering of souls, for *multitudes* of poor souls, and for many that I thought were the children of God, *personally*, in many distant places. I was in such agony, from sun half an hour high, till near dark, that I was all over wet with sweat.[10]

For two years, he traveled by horse, foot, or canoe, to different Indian tribes with little help and success. He describes his situation at one point in 1743,

> I live in the most lonesome wilderness; have but one single person to converse with, that can speak English. ...I have no fellow-Christian to whom I might unbosom myself, or lay open my spiritual sorrows;...I live poorly with regards to the comforts of life: most of my diet consists of boiled corn, hasty-pudding, &c. I lodge on a bundle of straw, my labor is hard and extremely difficult, and I have little appearance of success to comfort me.[11]

In spite of this, he endures and gives himself to continual prayer for breakthrough. A snapshot of his entries in the summer of 1744 is enough to see this.

> June 26: In prayer my soul was enlarged, and my faith drawn into sensible exercise; was enabled to cry to God for my poor Indians; and though the work of their conversion appeared impossible with man, yet with God I saw all things were possible.
> June 27: Saw, with great certainty, that the arm of the Lord must be revealed, for the help of these poor heathen,...Spent most of the time, while riding, in lifting up my heart for grace and assistance.
> June 28: Spent the morning...in fervent prayer for my Indians, that God would set up his kingdom among them, and bring them into his Church....The Lord helped me to plead with him for it.[12]

His prayer life never seems to dissipate, but grows in faith and power through trials, often setting aside days for prayer and fasting. In December 19, 1744, we see him continuing in the same spirit: "Spent a great part of the day in prayer to God for the outpouring of his Spirit on my poor people;...I had much freedom, five or six times in the day, in prayer and praise, and felt a weighty concern upon my spirit for the salvation of those precious souls, and the enlargement of the Redeemer's kingdom among them."[13]

That same month, he writes about his desire to live in the presence of God, "The Lord knows how I long for that world, where they rest not day nor night, saying, Holy, holy, holy is the Lord God Almighty."[14]

Little did he know that the day of victory and salvation was about to be loosed through the ministry of suffering and intercession that God had given him. In the summer of 1745, the heavens began to open in one of the most extraordinary outpourings of the Spirit. He shares in his public journal how he began to minister to the Indians at Crossweeksung in New Jersey at the Forks of Delaware. First, we see them showing great interest in the gospel, some even receiving Christ, and increasingly God is convicting and drawing them. Then the day of power, August 8, he writes:

> I preached to the Indians; their number was about 65 persons, men, woman, and children;...There was much visible concern among them while I was discoursing publicly; but afterwards when I spoke to one and another more particularly, whom I perceived under much concern, the power of God seemed to descend upon the assembly "like a rushing mighty wind," and with an astonishing energy bore down all before it.
>
> I stood amazed at the influence that seized the audience almost universally, and could compare it to nothing more aptly than the irresistible force of a mighty torrent or swelling deluge, that with its insupportable weight and pressure bears down and sweeps before it whatever is in its way. Almost all persons of all ages were bowed down with concern together, and scarce one was able to withstand the shock of this surprising operation.[15]

He goes on to describe how drunkards, murderers, and sorcerers were in that meeting:

> All were almost universally praying and crying for mercy in every part of the house, and many out of doors, and numbers could neither go nor stand. Their concern was so great, each one for himself, that none seemed to take any notice of those about them, but each prayed freely for himself....
>
> ...Methought this had a near resemblance to the day of God's power mentioned Josh. x. 14. For I must say, I never saw any day like it in all respects: It was a day wherein I am persuaded the Lord did much to destroy the kingdom of darkness among this people.[16]

Brainerd shows that a life of prayer is necessary for missionaries. He also shows us the connection of prayer and breakthrough among the unreached.

Return to the Prayer Room

The next revolution in missions will not be through new methodologies or breakthroughs in anthropology; it will be through a return to the prayer room. There are many expressions of this—a local church building where believers can gather continually to seek the Lord, house-to-house prayer gatherings, campus prayer rooms, prayer mountains, or citywide centers where sustained day and night worship and prayer continue, all in expectation of the harvest and the coming of the Lord. As the Church lifts up sustained and continual prayer for all nations, God will pour out his Spirit in an unprecedented way for his glory and salvation among all peoples. As we lift up his name in continual praise, he will lift up the poor, the broken, and the destitute of the earth. He will release prophecy, dreams, visions, and the power of the Holy Spirit in unparalleled ways as his people press into united and continual fasting and prayer (Acts 2:17-18).

I went to Bible school at the International House of Prayer in Kansas City. At the time of this writing, they have continued 15 years in day and night prayer and worship. During one of their annual conferences in downtown Kansas City, Corey Russell, one of the leaders of the House of Prayer, was preaching in the conference center. A hot dog vender from the city who was having a really bad day came into the room to just to sit down for a minute. He was a very committed Muslim from Egypt, had made Hajj (pilgrimage), and also acted at one point as a religious judge in his Middle Eastern community. By God's sovereignty, he ended up listening in on Corey's preaching. As he rested in the back of the room, not really sure what to think, suddenly the presence of God came over him and he began to shake and cry. He had never experienced anything like this, but knew that God was encountering him.

Someone sitting next to him in the back of the conference room, saw what was happening to him, and invited him to attend church that Sunday. After hearing about a great financial need he was facing, related to a vehicle accident, the church decided to take up an offering for him. They raised several thousand dollars for him on the spot. He was overwhelmed by the love of these people, and could not comprehend that Christians would treat a Muslim in this way. He gave his life to Jesus.

During this time, he began to attend a small group my wife and I were a part of. We packed about ten people into our small bathroom and baptized this former sheikh in the bathtub of our one-bedroom apartment. As he was coming out of the water, we all began to pray and declare God's purpose over his life. The Holy Spirit seemed to fill the room with an almost electric atmosphere. This man, who never even heard of the charismatic gifts, began to sputter and cry out in other tongues.

I started meeting with him regularly for discipleship, and had no idea what to say to a middle-aged former Muslim. I knew nothing about the Qur'an, and he knew nothing about the Bible! But it was during this year that I began to develop a burden for Muslims. This man has continued to trust Jesus as his savior and Lord to this day. He cries every time I see him over how much God has loved him. I believe the unique way in which God apprehended the heart of this former Muslim is directly related to the constant prayer that was the center of our community at IHOP-KC.

End Time Prayer

This is the pattern we find in the Scriptures; when the Church presses into the Holy Spirit through prayer, God moves in power and creates breakthrough in mission. It is common today to hear of Muslims coming to Christ through dreams and visions. It should be expected that when the Church does Acts chapter 1 (devotion to prayer), God does Acts chapter 2 (the outpouring of the Holy Spirit with dreams and visions). David Garrison has shown that from the advent of Islam until the 20th century, there were only two Muslim movements to Christ in the Islamic world. Yet in the 20th and 21st centuries, particularly in the last twenty years, there has been a major advance:

> Not until the end of the 19th century, twelve and a half centuries after the death of Muhammad, did we find the first voluntary movements of Muslims to Christ that numbered at least 1,000 baptisms....
>
> ...But then, in the final two decades of the 20th century, there was a surge of 11 additional movements....By the close of the 20th century, 1,368 years after the death of Muhammad, there had been a total of 13 movements of Muslim communities to faith in Jesus Christ....
>
> ...In only the first 12 years of the 21st century, an additional 69 movements to Christ of at least 1,000 baptized Muslim-background believers or 100 new worshiping fellowships have appeared. These 21st century movements are not isolated to one or two corners of the world. They are taking place throughout the House of Islam.[17]

Could it be that the impact being made in the Muslim world is related to a global rise of prayer?

In the last several decades, Operation World, Joshua Project, and other ministries have connected thousands of believers to pray specifically for unreached peoples and nations. In his recent work on prayer, Mike Bickle documents extensively a groundbreaking, unceasing, prayer movement happening all around the world.[18] The people of God are being stirred to pray like never before, and as the incense rises up to God night and day around the world, God will release Pentecost in places that have never experienced it.

In Luke 18, Jesus tells a parable about a persistent widow who never stops crying out for the intervention of an unjust judge. Jesus then juxtaposes this with the position of the Elect at the end of the age and says, "And will not God give justice to his elect, who cry to him day and night? Will he delay long over them? I tell you, he will give justice to them speedily. Nevertheless, when the Son of Man comes, will he find faith on earth?" (Luke 18:7-8). The phrase "when the Son of Man comes" puts this in an eschatological (end times) context. The kind of faith being referenced here is a persevering cry for justice, which includes salvation of the lost and deliverance of the oppressed, as well as judgment upon the wicked. Jesus is telling us the value of persistent prayer at the end of the age. Peter also speaks about the importance of prayer as the saints wait for the coming of the Lord, "The end of all things is at hand; therefore be self-controlled and sober-minded for the sake of your prayers" (1 Peter 4:7). Prayer is important because the end is at hand. Therefore, be holy, so that your prayers will not be ineffective.

The Bible calls the Church to unceasing prayer across the earth before the Lord returns; a great measure of prayer that will usher a multitude of souls into the kingdom of God.

Prayer in Africa

Christianity in Africa is saturated with the value of prayer. Prayer mountains, prayer rooms, and prayer altars cover the landscape of Sub-Saharan Africa. Without fail, every Friday night, all over the continent, there are overnight prayer meetings, and throughout the week there are lunch hour prayer gatherings. Maybe this fire for prayer is the reason why there are more believers in Africa today than people in America? Part of the legacy God is giving to the African Church is that it will be known for great prayer.

South Africa lead the way for the largest single prayer gathering in human history, "The Global Day of Prayer," which first started as a day of solemn prayer in a stadium in Capetown. The idea soon spread, and the next year towns and cities all over South Africa participated. In 2006, it was launched in all 56 countries in Africa. Stadiums were full all over Africa on the Day of Pentecost as multitudes were confessing sin and crying out for global revival. Finally, it was launched as a day for the Church to stand in unity before the Lord around the world. Hundreds of millions with more than 220 nations would participate in the largest organized prayer event ever.

This great spirit of prayer in Africa is why 24/7 prayer centers are the heart of every missions base that *Send56* develops. Each prayer center works together with local churches fulfilling the call of Christ to be a "House of Prayer for all nations." The prayer center is also the context for training missionaries in lifestyles devoted to Christ through prayer.

The House of Prayer Begins With Me

It is very easy to get lost as I speak of "day and night," and big concerted efforts of organized prayer, and to miss a very personal invitation from the Lord. Many do not really know how to practically get involved in reaching the unreached. But you can get involved right now because God hears you. Prayer is the greatest way to get involved in the Great Commission, whether in your closet, at your church, or at a prayer center. Pray for the nations. Get informed and get involved through personal intercession. My desire is to see believers from the West praying for Native missionaries in the field. Imagine a unified army of those going and those behind them praying. The house of prayer for all nations begins with you, and it begins right now.

1. Anderson, Phil. *Lord of the Ring: In Search of Count Von Zinzendorf.* Bethany House, 2007. 154.
2. *Count Zinzendorf.* Comenius Foundation; 2000. DVD.
3. Greenfield, John. "Chapter 1: A Modern Pentecost." In *Power from on High. The Two Hundredth Anniversary of the Great Moravian Revival.* pdf. http://www.path2prayer.com/site/1/docs/Greenfield_Power_From_on_High_complete.pdf Accessed January 22, 2015.
4. *Count Zinzendorf.* Comenius Foundation; 2000. DVD.
5. Hutton, Joseph Edmund. "Chapter IV. LIFE AT HERRNHUT." In *A History of the Moravian Church.* Kindle ed. London, 1909. 2nd ed. Public Domain Book. Prepared by John Bechard.
6. Bounds, Edward M. "Chapter 1: Prayer and Faith." In *The Necessity of Prayer.* Grand Rapids, Mich.: Christian Classics Ethereal Library, 1929.
7. Bounds, Edward M. "Chapter 3: Prayer and Trust." In *The Necessity of Prayer.* Grand Rapids, Mich.: Christian Classics Ethereal Library, 1929.
8. Edwards, Jonathan. "Part 1: From His Birth, To The Time When He Began To Study For The Ministry." In *The Life and Diary of David Brainerd with Notes and Reflections.* Kindle ed.
9. See 8.
10. Edwards, Jonathan. "Part 2. Study of Divinity Until Licensed To Preach." In *The Life and Diary of David Brainerd with Notes and Reflections.*
11. Edwards, Jonathan. "Part 5: From His Beginning To Instruct The Indians, To His Ordination." In *The Life and Diary of David Brainerd with Notes and Reflections.*

12. Edwards, Jonathan. "Part 6: From His Ordination Till He First Began To Preach At Crossweeksung." In *The Life and Diary of David Brainerd with Notes and Reflections*.

13. See 12.

14. See 12.

15. Brainerd, David. "Part 1: From A.D. 1745 June 19th to Nov. 4th, At Crossweeksung And The Forks Of Delaware." In *The Journal of David Brainerd*. Kindle ed.

16. See 15.

17. Garrison, David. "Chapter 1: Something Is Happening" In *A Wind in the House of Islam: How God Is Drawing Muslims around the World to Faith in Jesus Christ*. Kindle ed. Monument, CO: WIGTake Resources, 2014.

18. Bickle, Mike. "Chapter 28: The Global Prayer Movement Today." In *Growing in Prayer: A Real-life Guide to Talking with God*. Lake Mary, Florida 32746: Passio, Charisma House Book Group, 2014.

7

Global Partners in the Great Commission

Africa remains the most economically impoverished continent on the earth.[1] A majority of the population live on less than $5,000 a year, without adequate power or access to clean water. Most African people have no socio-political power. It is beyond the scope of this book to speak of the societal and political challenges Africans have faced over the centuries, including slavery, genocide, colonialism, dictatorships, and tribal feuds. Colonial boundaries set in the twentieth century created large-scale problems, lumping different tribes together and separating other tribes with invisible boundaries that never existed previously. Those in power often come from a particular tribe, and are resented by others within their country as they dole out position, money, and land to their own kin. Africa is slowly overcoming these massive difficulties, but it is not a simple or fast process. These circumstances perpetuate the cycle of corruption and poverty.

But Africa is changing. Rural peoples are moving to cities and becoming professionals. Education and technology are deeply impacting lives all over Africa. Many people, even in rural areas, have a cell phone and know how to use the internet. Colonial boundaries are becoming less strict and alliances like the East African Union are making it possible for people to cross borders without having to immigrate and pay fees. This is strengthening trade and building economies. Sub-Saharan Africa is also generally very friendly to Europe and America, and contains rich natural resources for trade. Most people don't know about these positive developments in Africa because they have never heard about them. Good news is rarely sensational enough for the media.

We also rarely hear about the amazing and vibrant believing community in many parts of Africa. The gospel has been burning like wild fire for more than a hundred years. It is bearing fruit; shifting the very foundations of societies. A staggering five-hundred *million* people have come to some level of faith and allegiance to Jesus over the last hundred years. There can be no doubt that Africa has a major destiny in the economy of heaven.

One cannot read James 2:5 and doubt its implications for the poorest continent, "Listen, my beloved brothers, has not *God chosen those who are poor in the world* to be rich in faith and heirs of the kingdom, which he has promised to those who love him?" God has an astounding plan for the African people. God chooses the poor and uses them to shift history and participate in his saving purpose. I believe God is choosing to do a mighty work in and through the African Church, and there are amazing possibilities right now for global partnership. Those from Global North nations have a dynamic opportunity to strengthen and support the missionaries God is raising up in Africa.

God often lifts up the most despised, neglected, and even oppressed people and puts them on the front lines of his glorious redemptive purpose. When the children of Israel cried out to the LORD because of the oppression of the Midianites, God chose the least likely candidate and said, "The LORD is with you, O mighty man of valor....Go in this might of yours and save Israel from the hand of Midian" (Judges 6:12, 14). Gideon was shocked; why would God choose him? "Please, Lord, how can I save Israel? Behold, my clan is the weakest in Manasseh, and I am the least in my father's household" (Judges 6:15).

Why did God chose the weakest in Israel to bring forth his saving purpose? A clue is found after Gideon gathers an army of 22,000 men by the spring of Harod preparing to face the Midianites for battle. The Lord tells Gideon, "The people with you are too many for me to give the Midianites into their hand, *lest Israel boast over me, saying, 'My own hand has saved me'*" (Judges 7:2). Most know the story of how the Lord commands Gideon to reduce the army until there are only three hundred men left. It is this weak army that the Lord uses to defeat the Midianites, and to bring peace to Israel. God dignifies the weak and glorifies himself.

In the same way, the Lord brought forth his Son into the world. Jesus was born in humility and poverty. The king of heaven came in obscurity, laid in a manger with the animals, to an insignificant Jewish family. "Can anything good come out of Nazareth?" they said (John 1:46). It is this poor Jewish man who destroyed the works of darkness and brought salvation to the world. The meek one conquered sin; the meek one will inherit the earth. He did not conquer through worldly might or riches, but through a humble life. He was the servant of all. He became poor so that we might become rich in him. God uses the poor. God is using beloved brothers and sisters from Africa to bring salvation to the nations.

Two missionaries from Uganda were sent to a rural area in South Sudan. They arrived with little more than the clothes on their back and a few personal items. The only place they were able to stay was in the compound of a soldier who was away from home. It was a simple African compound with several mud huts, but was overgrown and unused. They cleaned it up, put their mats on the ground, and called it home. There was not much for cookware, so they made a stove with the local clay and used it for cooking. Immediately, they began to do evangelism and prayer in the mornings. People from the local tribes became interested in their message, and several gave their lives to Christ. The people getting saved were rural shepherds, some only knowing how to barter animals for their goods, rather than use regular currency. This did not stop them from beginning a church. The missionaries were obtaining favor with the local people. The elders of the area invited them to eat with them, and fed them delicacies like cow head! They were also given an area on someone else's land where they could begin the church. Having few resources was no hindrance to them. They decided to begin praying under a tree. Within the first several months, these two men planted a church that is growing and thriving. They are now expanding into other villages which have no churches.

At the same time that Africa has been going through dramatic difficulties, and many countries in Africa, since independence, have actually reversed in economic wealth, North America and Europe have galvanized their place at the top, owning more than a 60% share in global household wealth. North America contains the highest average wealth in the world. A whopping 32% is held by 6% of the global population. Africa contains the least share in global wealth, coming in at around 2%, yet with a population of 12% (one billion people). Africa has the highest concentration of countries in the world with an average household income (if wealth is spread out evenly per adult) of $5,100,[2] compared to North America at $340,300 per adult.

Asking Why

This massive contrast between the Global North and Africa inevitably makes us ask *why*. As an American living in East Africa, I often wrestle with the topic of fairness in my heart. Why was I born into relative wealth? Why was my friend born in a poor village, where he lacks basic amenities and struggles just to feed himself and his family? Why is it that I am able to give my children milk and sugar and vitamin-enriched foods while many African families cannot? Why can I afford to live in a house with plumbing, running water, and electricity, while my friend has none of these and is trying, by all means, just to give his kids food and education? Why is Africa so poor? Can I make a difference? The only place I can find some sense of an answer to this question is from God. It is not enough to simply look at the circumstances of the world and conclude that it is their fault because they have not embraced good economics. It is possible to trace some of the reasons, as we have done briefly, why there is more well-being in the Global North than in Africa, but all such answers fall short of the complete truth.

Only the Scriptures provide us the full answer to the question why.

God's sovereignty is at the center of global inequality. He says to Samuel, "The LORD makes poor and makes rich; he brings low and he exalts. He raises up the poor from the dust; he lifts the needy from the ash heap to make them sit with princes and inherit a seat of honor. For the pillars of the earth are the LORD's, and on them he has set the world" (1 Samuel 2:7-8). God alone determines whether America and Europe will prosper and whether Asia and Africa will not, and at any moment he can turn the tables. God has good purposes in allowing these discrepancies, and we will take a brief moment to search them out.

Poverty Is Not Eternal

First, we must see that there is nothing in Scripture that glorifies poverty. Poverty is not good, and it is not part of God's eternal purpose, "A rich man's wealth is his strong city; the poverty of the poor is their ruin" (Proverbs 10:5). Some people wrongly assume that there is some kind of essential value or holiness in being poor, and that is simply wrong. As scholar, Craig Blomberg concludes in his in-depth study on possession in the Bible, "Material possessions are a good gift from God meant for his people to enjoy."[3] One of the results of the new community of believers in the book of Acts was that, "there was not a needy person among them" (Acts 4:34). This was the result of the profound impact the gospel had on their hearts. Prosperity came to the believers as they lived out Sermon on the Mount values, sharing their possessions with those in the community who had need. The gospel should impact the economic health of a believing community.

This is not to say that we should embrace the so called *prosperity gospel,* which has become so prevalent in much of America, Africa, and the Global South. This doctrine basically says that God promises material prosperity (riches) to those who receive Christ as savior. Usually, this gospel comes wrapped in dominion theology, which wrongly assumes the kingdom of God has already fully arrived on earth. It also places the Christian's hope in worldly pleasures, power, and possessions, rather than in the future kingdom of Christ and its reward. It often assumes God does not call his servants to humility and suffering, and motivates people to avoid the cost of discipleship, leaving them perpetually immature. This, coupled with the *word of faith, name it and claim it* teaching, causes poor believers to wonder if they have any faith, or whether their economic status is an indication of God's favor (or the lack there of) on their lives. A small number of successful prosperity preachers live pompously, calling others to give, while they themselves reap the benefits. These lies should be confronted, but not at the cost of overcompensating by glorifying poverty. The destruction that poverty brings to the lives of real families around the world is not good, and God does not want his people to be poor forever. What then could be the purpose of God in allowing poverty and imbalance in the world?

Poverty Exposes Our Need for God

Poverty exposes the need we have for God in all things. The world and everything good in it is a gift from God to man. He has given life, breath, ability, and yes, money. But when the wicked obtain wealth, they often cast God off, thinking they are rich by their own powers. Like a child who receives money from a parent to buy something, and then quickly goes bragging to a friend about how rich they are, they are in fact no richer or less dependent than they were before.

Many Scriptures emphasize this point when they warn about wealth. They do not say that riches are essentially evil, but that they are a major cause of forgetting God. From the wisdom of Solomon, "give me neither poverty nor riches; feed me with the food that is needful for me, lest I be full and deny you and say, 'Who is the LORD?' or lest I be poor and steal and profane the name of my God" (Proverbs 30:8b-9). Jesus warns us about the deceitfulness of riches, "but the cares of the world and the deceitfulness of riches and the desires for other things enter in and choke the word, and it proves unfruitful" (Mark 4:19). Paul warns that it is through the love of money that some have wondered spiritually, "For the love of money is a root of all kinds of evils. It is through this craving that some have wandered away from the faith and pierced themselves with many pangs" (1 Tim 6:10).

The only thing that separates you or me from being in the position of the destitute is the unmerited grace of God, which means that all are in fact poor. I did not lift a finger to be born into a successful society, or into a household with a loving family. If I did not control or order my circumstances the way they are, and was unable to choose whether I would be born an orphan or in wealthy circumstances, than I am utterly dependent on sovereign grace. If I am dependent, then I am poor. If we do not acknowledge our poverty apart from God, we cannot be rich in Christ. The faith that truly embraces the gospel includes the acknowledgment of poverty or dependence on God in all of life. This is why the Psalmist declares, "as for me, I am poor and needy, but the Lord takes thought for me" (Psalm 40:17), "but I am poor and needy;

hasten to me, Oh God! You are my help and my deliverer" (Psalm 70:5), and "incline your ear oh Lord and answer me, for I am poor and needy" (Psalm 86:1).

This acknowledgement is required in the gospel, and is the reason Jesus says that "only with difficulty will a rich person enter the kingdom of heaven" (Matthew 19:23). The materially rich often do not think that they need God, and cannot understand their own poverty apart from him. In fact, it is impossible for anyone who does not acknowledge their own powerlessness and poverty to enter the kingdom, "blessed are the poor in spirit, for theirs is the kingdom of heaven" (Matthew 5:3). The problem with those who think they are rich because of material possessions, people who trust in Godless materialism, is that they do not know that they are poor. This is illustrated in Jesus' warning to the Church in Laodicea:

> So, because you are lukewarm, and neither hot nor cold, I will spit you out of my mouth. For you say, *I am rich*, I have prospered, and *I need nothing*, not realizing that you are wretched, pitiable, poor, blind, and naked. I counsel you to buy from me gold refined by fire, so that you may be rich, and white garments so that you may clothe yourself and the shame of your nakedness may not be seen, and salve to anoint your eyes, so that you may see. (Revelation 3:16–18)

Notice that the materially rich become aware of their own spiritual state by imagining the wretched, pitiable, poor, blind, and naked. When we see people in this material state, we should not imagine that we are essentially different. All are poor apart from God. Those in Laodicea were not aware of this because of their worldly possessions; they did not know their need. They are commanded to essentially repent through the acknowledgment of their own poverty, so that they might receive true spiritual blessing from God. They must buy from him what money cannot afford.

The Proverbs show that the danger of riches is in trusting them, "whoever trusts in riches will fall, but the righteous will flourish like a green leaf" (Prov. 11:28). Believers are called to keep themselves free from the love of money, and instead to trust in the Lord who will never leave them, "Keep your life free from love of money, and be content with what you have, for he has said, 'I will never leave you nor forsake you'" (Hebrews 13:5). Antithetical to loving and trusting God is loving and trusting money. "You cannot serve God and money," Jesus said (Matthew 6:24).

Though we possess power and material wealth, we are still utterly nothing without God. God has chosen to make the poor rich in him. In this way, the materiality poor do have an advantage. Often, the poor realize their need of God because they are more acutely aware of their own lack of power. So, although there is pain in poverty, there is also a hidden blessing for those who gain the right perspective. The poor can more easily come to trust God for provision and even vindication, which God freely provides to those who trust him. As the Psalmist says, "in your goodness, oh God, you provide for the needy" (Psalm 68:10), and "he has distributed freely; he has given to the poor" (Psalm 112:9). Poverty makes all aware of their utter dependence upon God. Being "poor in spirit" is the acknowledgment of this.

Poverty Reveals the Heart

Poverty exposes the hearts of both the wicked and the righteous. It is not skin color or ethnicity that are the greatest dividers in the world, but rather greed and pride. Class divisions between rich and the poor seem to be more toxic than racism or tribalism. Blomberg, commenting on the parable of the Good Samaritan, says, "Then, as now, in many cultures rich and poor were also virtual enemies, with the former shunning the latter as much as possible."[4] On the part of the poor, there is hatred and mistrust of the rich (often for good reason) and a coveting of what they have. On the other hand, the rich tend to despise the poor and oppress them, denigrating them as a lesser class of humanity. God allows poverty to expose both the covetous and the haughty, and to give chance for the righteous to be distinguished by his self-giving love through a new spirit of reconciliation.

Wealth gained through exploitation of the poor, or with indifference to the plight of the needy, is strongly condemned in the Bible. Those who waste their wealth on exalting their own pride and pleasure and oppressing the poor are warned, "Come now, you rich, weep and howl for the miseries that are coming upon you. Your riches have rotted and your garments are moth eaten. Your gold and silver have corroded, and their corrosion will be evidence against you and will eat your flesh like fire" (James 5:1-3). These rich were most likely wealthy land owners who were exploiting and oppressing poor believers.

Jesus' encounter with the rich young ruler is also telling. The man's heart is exposed through his unwillingness to lay down his money in order to follow Christ, which shows that he did not discern the worth of Christ. Jesus tells him, "One thing you still lack. Sell all that you have and distribute to the poor, and you will have treasure in heaven; and come, follow me" (Luke 18:22). Riches were more valuable to this young man than Christ. The solution? Unhindered, extravagant giving. The surest way for those who are blessed materially to be free from the love of money is to share as much as possible with those in need. Radical giving is the practical life of the redeemed. The rich man's heart was revealed by his wealth. He could not see that Christ was more valuable than his bank account.

At the same time, the poor are not exempt from criticism. Laziness and sloth are connected to poverty: "A little sleep, a little slumber, a little folding of the hands to rest, and poverty will come upon you like a robber, and want like an armed man" (Proverbs 6:10). The Bible does not advocate for enabling a lazy person who will not work, as Paul's statement makes clear: "For even when we were with you, we would give you this command: If anyone is not willing to work, let him not eat. For we hear that some among you walk in idleness, not busy at work, but busybodies. Now such persons we command and encourage in the Lord Jesus Christ to do their work quietly and to earn their own living" (2 Thessalonians 3:10–12). The poor have to fight hard against covetousness, and remember that their worth does not come from the acquisition of money or power, but from the Lord. Dependence on Christ, hard work, and contentment are to be sought after.

Jesus is both the example of the righteous rich and the faithful poor. In his riches, he existed with God in eternal joy and happiness. Then he agreed with the Father's love for the poor and became poor, in the incarnation, for his eternal saving purpose. Because Jesus became poor and gave his life for the sins of the world, he is also highly exalted in eternal glory. This, then, is how the rich of this world should position their heart, always willing to give up their wealth for God's redemptive purpose. The rich are called to embrace poverty of spirit, and to associate with the humble in order to participate with the heart of God. The rich are called to share their wealth through giving to the poor, and in this way embrace poverty of spirit and enter into agreement with God's agenda for redemption and the lifting of the poor: "Is not this the fast that I choose: to loose the bonds of wickedness, to undo the straps of yoke, to let the oppressed go free, and to break every yoke? Is it not to share your bread with the hungry and bring the homeless poor into your house; when you see the naked, to cover him, and not to hide yourself from your own flesh?" (Isaiah 58:6-7).

God is the lifter of the needy, and the destroyer of the proud. The faithful poor experience his gift of provision and grace as they trust him with all of their heart. He also invites the faithful rich to participate in the grace of his self-giving love by giving and becoming his agents of relief. Poverty and wealth is a weighing and testing of humanity, and this is why "you always have the poor with you" (Matthew 26:11).

God Demonstrates His Glory Through the Poor

God reveals his glory as the all-sufficient provider and defender of the poor. Christ the King will come and vindicate the poor by delivering them out of oppression, "If a king faithfully judges the poor, his throne will be established forever" (Proverbs 29:14). Jesus will establish justice in the earth, and will judge the rich and the poor according to their heart. This is how King Jesus deals with the poor, "For you know the grace of our Lord Jesus Christ, that though he was rich, yet for your sake he became poor, so that you by his poverty might become rich" (2 Corinthians 8:9). This means that he chooses the poor. Jesus quoted Isaiah when he launched his ministry and said, "The Spirit of the Lord is upon me, because he has anointed me to proclaim the gospel to the poor" (Luke 4:18). The gospel is proclaimed to the poor, and if we want it to be for us, then we also need to acknowledge our poverty.

The gospel is meant to lift the poor out of their brokenness by seating them with Christ and involving them in his prophetic and redemptive purpose. The glory of God's self-giving love is revealed in his election of the unworthy, unprivileged, and despised. His glory is demonstrated when he works on behalf of the poor who trust in him amidst the wise and powerful of this world. Consider the message of 1 Corinthians 1:26-31:

> For consider your calling, brothers: not many of you were *wise* according to worldly standards, not many were *powerful*, not many were of *noble birth*. But God chose what is foolish in the world to shame the wise; God chose what is weak in the world to shame the strong; *God chose* what is *low* and *despised* in the world, even *things that are not,* to bring to nothing things that are*, so that no human being might boast in the presence of God*. And because of him you are in Christ Jesus, who became to us wisdom from God, righteousness and sanctification and redemption, so that, as it is written, 'Let the one who boasts, boast in the Lord.' (1 Corinthians 1:26–31)

God is orchestrating his glorious purpose through the gospel in such a way that he alone will receive the glory for its fulfillment. The whole context of this passage is the message of the cross, and the kind of messengers that he has chosen to carry it forward. According to worldly standards, many of those the Lord has chosen are foolish (uneducated), and those not of noble birth (the rich). God has chosen the humble to carry out his purpose that he might receive the glory for everything in the end. When he demonstrates his self-giving love to the poor and his sufficiency for those who trust in him, he exalts the glory of his mercy. The poor will be dignified and God will be glorified!

God is going to equalize all before his glory. He will cause all to know that wealth and power and importance in this age have nothing to do with his assessment or judgment of mankind. The shrewdest politician or the wealthiest businessman will not be able to manipulate God's judgment of their life. There is no string they can pull at the judgment seat, and no person they can call upon to help them. The pauper and the king will stand side by side at the judgment seat of Christ and receive the reward for what they did in the body, whether good or bad. And to whom much is given, much will be required. To the degree that someone is born into wealth, privilege, and opportunity, God will account for whether they used what they were given to uphold his cause among the poor and further his name and glory in the earth, or whether they wasted it on their own desires.

Global Partnership in the Great Commission

There is yet another reason for the great financial divide between the Global North and Global South. It creates an opportunity for unity in the global Church. We can and we must join hands in the glorious purpose of completing the task of world missions. God will not allow the Church in the richest nations to boast and say "we did it!" because they had all the money and the workers. The Western missions complex is part of a global and multicultural initiative, and the frontier workers who are preaching and church planting are now largely not from the Global North but from nations in the Global South. Western missionaries need the help of those in the developing world who are dynamic and effective in preaching the gospel, and who are closer in proximity to the unreached. At the same time, those in the developing nations will not be able to claim, "we did it!" because to a great extent they are going to be helped by the churches in the Global North. More experienced agencies and workers are needed to advise and help the missions movement in Africa to reach its potential. In the end, all people will say "God did it!" as we worked together in his purpose for the redemption of the nations through the name of Christ.

The Church in the Global North has a powerful opportunity to serve the missions movement by giving financially to help support missionaries that God is calling from the Global South. We can help fund our brothers and sisters in Africa to preach the gospel. What Paul says in 2 Corinthians 8:14-15 is noteworthy, "*your abundance* at the present time *should supply their need,* so that their abundance may supply your need, that there may be fairness. As it is written, "Whoever gathered much had nothing left over, and whoever gathered little had no lack." Paul is asking the Church in different parts of the Mediterranean world to share in a relief fund that will help the poor in Jerusalem. When the Church in Macedonia cannot afford to give, the Church in Corinth can fill up what is lacking so that the work can be accomplished. This promotes fairness and equality. He does not want it to be compulsory, but from the heart of each believer as they respond to the Holy Spirit (2 Corinthians 9).

In the same way, believers from the Global North can fill up what is lacking in the ability of the Church in the developing world to fund the movement of the gospel to unreached peoples. We can humble ourselves and serve the native missions movement. In this way, there can be an expression of global unity, love, and humility. It is a humbling thing to stand behind our brethren who are laboring in the field in some of the most difficult nations in the world.

Native missionaries can often go places where someone from America or Europe cannot as easily get to, and thereby supply the need to spread the gospel to the unreached. Both John and Paul speak of those who send or give as being partakers and partners in the missionary task itself. Romans 10:15 says, "And how are they to preach unless they are sent? As it is written, 'How beautiful are the feet of those who preach the good news!'" The one who sends is vitally connected and important to the work of missions. Missionaries cannot preach unless they are sent.

Third John is even more explicit. John encourages Gaius to send off those who were with him:

> Beloved, it is a faithful thing you do in all your efforts for these brothers, strangers as they are, who testified to your love before the church. You will do well to *send them* on their journey in a manner worthy of God. For *they have gone out for the sake of the name,* accepting nothing from the Gentiles. Therefore *we ought to support people like these,* that we may be *fellow workers* for the truth. (3 John 5-8)

These visitors were missionaries who had "gone out for the sake of the name" and were not receiving support from the people among whom they were laboring. The Gentiles will not pay missionaries to reach them! Therefore they needed help from the other believers. Even though Gaius did not know them very well, "strangers as they are," John encourages him to give to them. They have a good reputation from John, and were engaged in the labor of the gospel. John tells Gaius "we ought to support people like these that we may be fellow workers for the truth." What an amazing truth! The one who supports a missionary is a fellow worker with that missionary.

The Financial Advantage of Supporting Native Missionaries

It is worth expounding on what we briefly mentioned in chapter 3; supporting native missionaries is a cost effective strategy for reaching the unreached. Missionaries from Africa can be sent to the unreached for about 30 times less than the average missionary from America. Missionaries from the West on average take $30,000 to $65,000 a year for traveling and living costs. Contrast that with the $2,400 to $4,800 a year it can take to fully support a native missionary in the field, and you begin to see the potential. K.P. Yohannan, founder of Gospel for Asia, a ministry which has trained and supported thousands of native missionaries in India, made this point years ago in his book Revolution in World Missions:

> During a recent consultation on world evangelism, Western missionary leaders called for 200,000 new missionaries by the year 2000 in order to keep pace

> with their estimates of population growth. The cost of even a moderate missionary force would be a staggering 20 billion a year. When you realize that in 1996 North American Christians contributed just over 2.5 billion for missions, we are facing an astronomical fundraising effort. There has to be an alternative.[5]

For Yohannan, the alternative was for the Church in America and Europe to help fund native missionaries from Asia. And it's working. Thousands of churches are being planted in Asia by native missionaries with the partnership of their Global North brethren.

Blomberg also weighs in on this idea in Neither Poverty nor Riches, his scholarly work on a biblical theology of possession. After a full range of commentary on what the Bible says about wealth and poverty, he gives some comments of practical application for the individual believer living in the Western world:

> When we do give money to missions, we need to calculate the cost of sending short-term or long-term Westerners with what generally approximates to a western lifestyle, versus supporting and training indigenous leadership in areas that already have some kind of Christian work. Choosing the latter option would also help us to channel more missionary effort toward completely or largely unreached people groups.[6]

Of course, cost effectiveness is not the definitive argument for supporting native missionaries. It is simply one thing that should be considered when giving. Ultimately, the calling and effectiveness of each individual, not just how much it costs to support him or her, is what must be weighed. If you want to build a skyscraper, you don't pick someone off the street to be the architect just because it will cost less. If you do, the building probably won't stand very long. Rather, you choose someone who is able to do the task, even if it costs 30 times as much. So this is not an argument against supporting Western missionaries. There are strengths that Western missionaries bring to the table. It is not "either or" but "both and." All who are called should be sent!

Shouldn't Africa Send Its Own Missionaries?

Because the average income of someone in Sub-Saharan Africa is low, it is very difficult for the average pastor to receive financial income from ministry. This is not as much a problem in places that are already churched. Paul advised leaders, pastors, and missionaries to work with their own hands, as he sometimes did. Those doing ministry in areas which may already have a Christian presence should be encouraged to stay free from foreign dependence. But, if we are talking about missionaries who are crossing cultural boundaries to bring the gospel where there is no church, foreign funds are greatly advantageous. It is hard for African congregations to support their own pastors; it is even more difficult for them to send cross-cultural missionaries. When the majority of church members are struggling just to feed and educate their children, you can probably imagine that it is difficult for them to invest in cross-cultural missions.

Missionary training is equally challenging for most local churches. Affordable Bible schools are increasing and there are mobile training programs being offered, but these often lack the level of training that would adequately prepare someone for cross-cultural challenges, or on how to address the Islamic challenge in Africa. The Church in Africa needs training and funding that will serve the broader need of cross-cultural missions.

Send56

Someone may see the wisdom of supporting indigenous missionaries, but simply not know how or where to give. Making a connection with someone in another continent is not always easy, and verifying their work is an even harder process. This is the reason *Send56* exists: to serve the African missions movement.

We are making the connection between Western believers who want to see the unreached in Africa come to Christ, and the native missionaries who will carry out that commission with effectiveness. We develop discipleship schools which prepare missionaries to face the great challenge of Islam and cross-cultural missions. After completing the missions school, *Send56* mobilizes them into the unreached areas of Africa to plant churches in partnership with indigenous churches and leaders.

Maybe you have been awakened to the need of bringing the gospel to the lost who have no access to it, but you still feel the means of actually doing it is ambiguous and out of reach. Right now, it is possible to become a fellow worker in the Great Commission by helping *Send56* send out a missionary from Africa to this broken world. We want to see believers and churches all over America and Europe become involved through means of partnership and prayer.

Akam is from a rural tribe in the Horn of Africa. He grew up as a nominal Muslim, fearful of Allah's fierce judgment, but bound in his personal life. He was a drug addict who lived on the streets and wrestled to find meaning in his life. One day, he heard of a Christian woman from his tribe. She was known for praying for the sick in the name of Jesus and they would recover. It was through her ministry that he was drawn to Christ. After Akam accepted Christ, he experienced God's touch, and was delivered from his life of addiction. He soon found work, and continued fellowshipping with a small group of Christians from his own tribe. It was five months later when he was told about *Send56* and the School of Missions and Prayer.

Akam attended the training with a passion to learn about Christ and to be his servant in the nations. Christ gave all for him; he wanted to give all for Christ. Over two years, Akam learned how to study the Bible and how to teach and preach. He learned what it means to have a deep heart relationship with God; something he never had before. He also learned answers to hard questions he had heard about Christianity from Muslim teachers, and he was prepared to bring the gospel to his own Islamic culture.

After graduation, Akam got married and was sent to the Horn of Africa with his wife. They quickly impacted the rural Islamic community where they were working. They began to share about Christ with their neighbors, formed a Bible study, and started a ministry reaching out to impoverished children. In a nearby village, a small church was burned down by those opposed to the gospel, but that did not deter Akam and his wife from the work they were doing.

One day, a woman came to the church who had previously suffered a stroke and was paralyzed in part of her body. The believers prayed for her and she miraculously recovered! More Muslims began to come to Jesus. They decided that it was time to expand the fellowship and plant two more groups in nearby villages. They also decided it was time to preach the gospel openly and setup an open-air evangelistic meeting. After the meeting convened, a local Imam came to the church asking to see the pastor. He told them that after he heard their message he was drawn to give his life to Christ and to leave Islam. Along with this Imam, four others from the mosque came to the church and gave their lives to Jesus. This is the kind of fruit that native missionaries are bearing in the nations.

Akam and his wife are supported in their ministry through *Send56* by brethren from America. Who knows if this fruit would have come forth had it not been for the faithful giving of someone from another continent? Akam's family lives a very simple lifestyle by any standard, but they are producing great fruit for the kingdom of God. This is what global partnership is all about. Consider praying and asking the Lord whether you should also get involved and begin to support a native missionary (see appendix A). Together we can see thousands trained and sent to the harvest fields.

Many of today's gospel preachers are like Paul, "as sorrowful, yet always rejoicing; *as poor, yet making many rich;* as having nothing, yet possessing everything" (2 Corinthians 6:10). We can join hands with these men and woman of God to finish this great task. The goal is in our reach. Could we not give out of our abundance, so that workers in Africa can fulfill their calling in the gospel? We have a divine privilege to serve the African missions movement; the glorious chance to bring in the end-time harvest through partnership.

Imagine a grassroots army of believers from America and Europe, praying for and serving the African prayer and missions movement. This is the dream I am dreaming. What would God do with that kind of unity? There has never been such a dynamic opportunity to work together globally for the fulfillment of the Great Commission. Let's make the *must* of Jesus, the ambition of our lives, and bring the gospel to the ends of the earth, *together*.

1. Stierli, Mark, Anthony Shorrocks, James B. Davies, Rodrigo Lluberas, and Antonios Koutsoukis. *Global Wealth Report 2014* (Credit Suisse AG: Research Institute, September 19, 2014), accessed January 18, 2015. https://publications.credit-suisse.com/tasks/render/file/?fileID=60931FDE-A2D2-F568-B041B58C5EA591A4. PDF. 10-11, 24.
2. *Global Wealth Report 2014*. Also see Global Wealth Report 2012. https://publications.credit-suisse.com/tasks/render/file/index.cfm?fileid=88EE6EC8-83E8-EB92-9D5F39D5F5CD01F4. 11.
3. Blomberg, Craig L. *Neither Poverty nor Riches: A Biblical Theology of Material Possessions* (New Studies in Biblical Theology 7). Downers Grove, Illinois 60515: Inter Varsity Press, 2000. 243.
4. Blomberg, Craig L. *Neither Poverty nor Riches*. 117.
5. Yohannan, K. P. *Revolution in World Missions*. Rev. ed. Carrollton, TX: GFA Books, 2004. 148-149.
6. Blomberg, Craig L. *Neither Poverty nor Riches*. 251.

Appendix A

Sponsoring a Native Missionary

Sponsoring a native missionary is a fantastic way to get involved with reaching the lost of Africa. Through *Send56* you can adopt a missionary for just $25 per month. We give you a prayer card with the picture and testimony of your missionary and regular updates from their ministry. Each *Send56* base in Africa works together with the missionaries sending church, to provide them pastoral care and oversee their progress and fruitfulness on the missions field.

The missionaries of *Send56* go through two years of training in our School of Missions and Prayer (MAP). This school combines practical training and discipleship with theological education and apologetic preparation. We provide a particular focus on cross-cultural outreach and church planting. When you sponsor a missionary through *Send56* you are supporting a trained and vetted missionary from Africa to go to an unreached tribe (often Muslim) with the gospel, and partnering with us to fulfill the great commission

Your monthly gift goes toward their training; providing travel documents such as passports, visas, and work permits; transportation to the unreached areas; emergency medical help; and a monthly personal living allowance to cover necessities like housing and food. The actual cost to train and send a native missionary ranges from $200-$400 per month depending on the location where they are serving. When a sponsor gives $25 or more per month, we pair that person with other sponsors and are able to send a missionary. Many would love to give $50, $100, $200 or more and fully sponsor one or more missionaries. We welcome and ask people to do what they are able in the grace of God. Every gift is vital!

We encourage local churches to adopt a native missionary. This is a fantastic opportunity to begin sharing with your congregation about reaching the unreached, and it provides a dynamic opportunity to be involved in the Great Commission. I love when I see the picture of a native missionary on the wall of a local church, and have confidence that people are praying for the missionary and for the unreached!

One of our main goals is mobilizing the church to pray for the laborers going to the unreached. We encourage all those who adopt a native missionary to pray daily for that person, as they are really serving in the field, sometimes in dangerous circumstances and facing various difficulties. We want to see thousands of believers holding up these African missionaries before the Lord in daily intercession. Thank you for taking the time to pray and consider becoming a fellow worker with a native missionary today. Please see where to send your gift in the back of this book, or visit www.Send56.org.

Appendix B

Addressing Concerns about Foreign Funding of Nationals

I have come across some very valid concerns regarding transnational missions funding in various discussions on this topic. One point often made, which I agree with, is that foreign dependency can actually be detrimental to a church planting movement within a given people group. Also, there is fear that Western funds create an unhealthy culture of dependency in the Church in the developing world. The negative results of foreign money can be that indigenous believers in a given place develop an unhealthy quest for Western money as the motivation for ministry, rather than a sincere heart in serving God. Many countries in Africa are rife with examples of people who have misused funds or distorted information to obtain Western finances. There are nightmare stories of ministers who give bloated testimonies of their church networks, or who get churches from the West to send money for orphanages, only to find that they do not exist. Unfortunately, these are true stories.

It is equally true that lack of sufficient funding is a crippling factor for missions to unreached peoples. As much as we lament the horror stories, there are also just as many faithful native pastors and leaders who could absolutely use our support, and will use it well. Missions cannot happen without support, and there are thousands of native African missionaries who would go if they had the funding. I believe that honest and honorable native missionaries and pastors in the Global South far outnumber the dishonest. These men and women are just as worthy to receive funding as Western missionaries are.

Concerning whether foreign funds will hinder church planting movements, this is especially the case if money from the West is needed for multiplication or growth of the local churches. Foreign funds can serve, if given in the wrong way and in the wrong context, to foster laziness in the local believers, wherein they will be unwilling to work and establish the work without Western help. On the other hand, foreign funds, given in the right way and in the right context, can greatly help in sending workers to unreached peoples in the initial stages of church planting. Often, it is not a lack of passion that keeps people from going to the nations with the gospel, but a lack of money, and sometimes, knowledge of how to get there. Someone may feel the call to go, but lack the ability to pay for transportation or support their families in the place they would be going. We believe it is more than reasonable that an African missionary receive support that is equal to the standard of income the average person in Africa would earn.

Finally, some are afraid that if the economy is disrupted in America or elsewhere, then whatever work was done that was dependent on the West will be lost. The money will dry up and the work will have to end. For this reason, native missionaries should be self-sufficient and have a "tent-making" skill to support themselves on the mission field.

First, we need to acknowledge that most missionary work is dependent on voluntary giving. If we are talking about removing dependence from missions, then we are talking about closing shop for many amazing missions all over the world. Many depend on the free will giving of the body of

Christ. The unreached will not pay for people to come and evangelize them. Missions will have a need of funding as long as there are peoples who need the gospel. Wycliff, Campus Crusade, and YWAM are all support-based ministries that depend on gifts from churches in the West. Other missions organizations are connected to denominations, and the missionaries that are sent out from them are given support through the missions organization. In this case, funding is still obtained through the giving of church members. The vast majority of Western missionaries are receiving money from the West, which supports their efforts in other nations, and the vast majority are not working in areas that are unreached.

Consider that millions of dollars are spent to support short-term missionaries each year who are mostly involved in going to reached areas with the gospel. It is not uncommon for a team of about 15 American young people to raise upwards of $50,000 to visit a couple village churches, spend time with the poor, and do children's ministry. Usually, the team will make a donation to the local believers who are hosting them. These believers will be filled with joy at the small gift that went toward what is happening in their community, but it was just a fraction of the total cost of their plane tickets, hotel, and ground transportation that it took to bring the team to an already reached area. Fifty Thousand dollars can potentially fund 20 full-time native missionaries for a year on the field among the unreached.

I am not against short-term missions. It is very good for the American Church to send their young people onto the mission field to get real world ministry experience, and a short-term trip could potentially lead to a long-term missionary (not to mention that people get saved through these short term trips). I don't believe that God will run out of enough money to fund whatever work is done in his name. When you give, you will never lack the supply necessary to continue giving to the work of the gospel. We should not be so arrogant as to believe that the financial resources of heaven can be exhausted. We should also acknowledge that all missionary work is dependent in some sense on the giving of the Church. In this generation, most of the potential resources to fuel missions are found in the churches of the Global North. It is somewhat disingenuous to talk about the danger of dependency, when the American Church has thousands of dependent missionaries living in the Global South (they are not working in that country to support themselves financially). We seem to accept the validity of these missionaries being extra-locally funded without question, but when it comes to supporting native missionaries the knee-jerk reaction can be that the native worker must fully support his or herself.

The fear that ministry propped up by foreign funds will fail if the economy fails needs to be applied across the board. We should be concerned about the global economy. All missions will suffer as a result of a decline. At the same time, we must be confidant that God will provide for his workers until the coming of Christ. That is as sure as any rock solid foundation. The nations, all of them, will receive a witness, and God will continue to supply seed to the sower as long as there is a harvest to be reaped. It is also far more likely that a native missionary from Africa will be able to remain on the mission field if there were some kind of economic collapse.

But should missionaries work to support themselves in ministry? I think we need to bring into question the assumption that all foreign missionaries can be fully supported through tent-making without voluntary giving.

Paul was a tent-maker, but he was also given free will offerings to help in his mission. I believe that missionaries should do work along with their ministry activities. Tent-making skills are important for missionaries, but these skills do not take away the need for support. Some assume that empowering good businesses and business leaders who double as missionaries is the only way it should be done. I have seen problems with this first hand. Missions strategies that focus a lot of time on developing businesses can easily go off track and get distracted from preaching and church planting. Training people in how to do spreadsheets is valuable, but they also need to be trained how to study the Bible and make disciples. Businesses are meant to make a profit and can easily be mishandled. Many business plans have been implemented in the developing world with the intent to support missions work on the ground, and many have failed, wasting thousands of dollars and hours, because they never produce a profit. In America, only about 50 percent of small businesses continue after the first five years. Within ten years, the majority fail.

We need to have a realistic picture when developing missions strategies. I believe the best approach is a balanced one. We should help support the workers of the gospel financially, while also empowering them with skills and small businesses ideas that are tested and will be effective in the places they are going.

Until all nations have the word of God planted in their culture, and disciples are being made among all peoples, we will need the Church to sow finances into the work of sending missionaries. The one who preaches the gospel should live by the gospel, and is worthy of support whether they are American or Nigerian. It is not a matter of whether we *should* give money to help the missions movement in the Global South, but rather it is *how* do we do it in a healthy and accountable way. The goal should be to develop partnerships that do not rely on unhealthy dependency, discrimination, manipulation, or too much foreign control. We should also prioritize giving to those who are preaching the gospel and planting churches among the unreached peoples of the world, instead of where the Church is already established and self-sufficient. This would help to get churches in reached areas to take more ownership, and it would shift resources to where they are most desperately needed—in bringing the message of the gospel to those who have never heard it.

Send56 Stipulations

Send56 has developed a few key ways to combat these complications that can develop through transnational giving:

1. We support native missionaries to unreached peoples specifically. We do not fund pastors who are already pastoring people in areas that have been primarily reached. In order to qualify for missionary support, the worker must be going into an area where there are very few or no churches.

2. The missionary must have completed training in biblical studies and character development. Though you can never catch everything, in the intense discipleship environment, our experience is that someone with false motivations or bad character will be found out before they complete their two to three-year course.

3. Money should be given in a way that *empowers,* not controls. Temptation and error often enter financial situations where large sums must be designated to specific projects. Many people have been disappointed when funds are

misused. Our philosophy is to give someone monthly support for their cost of living on the ground. We do not track every penny they spend. Instead, we track fruitfulness in ministry and life. This instills dignity and freedom in a person who is trusted as an individual to spend money in appropriate ways. We are far more interested in supporting individuals who plant churches, than in supporting church buildings or projects. The resulting believing community takes responsibility for these projects.

4. Each missionary is trained with a tent-making skill and encouraged to work in order to supplement their costs in the field. This creates not only an income for the missionary to support himself, with the goal of coming off of international support, but is also a dynamic ministry opportunity in his or her community, especially in a place where an evangelist or Christian pastor would not be welcomed.

Appendix C

Should I Go?

My aim is not to discourage any Western Christians from becoming missionaries, nor is it to discourage Western donors from giving to them. What a hypocrite I would be! There is a great need for laborers of every nationality to go to the nations. Many unreached people groups are in need of those who will obey the simple command of Jesus: go into the world and preach the gospel. I have great respect for Western missions agencies that are mobilizing thousands from the Global North to reach the lost. All who are called must go!

Maybe as you are reading this you feel discouraged, as though asking people to serve and give to native missionaries in Africa means that one should not respond to the same Great Commission if they are from America or Europe. As if the West should no longer be involved in going but only be involved in sending. If you feel that discouragement from reading this, maybe that means you are called to go. When I read K. P. Yohonnan's book Revolution in World Missions ten years ago my heart burned within me. I knew that I was called to go to the nations and reach the Muslim world. The Lord had personally encountered me and put it on my heart to go. My wife and I immediately began to sponsor a native missionary in Asia through GFA as we also prepared for our own sending. Did your heart burn within you as you read this book? Then you may be called to give your life to the harvest.

At the same time, I ask you to consider and heed the many points in this book related to what the Great Commission is and how it should be carried out. If you are praying about going, consider going to the unreached, strive for purity, proclaim the testimony of Jesus, and do not love your own life. Understand that to be a missionary is to be entrusted with the word of Christ.

Many today do not want to give up their life when they go to new lands. They want to live half on the mission field and they want to live half where they came from; spending more time on social media than laboring to bring the gospel to the lost. Jesus said, "Truly, truly, I say to you, unless a grain of wheat falls into the earth and dies, it remains alone; but if it dies, it bears much fruit. Whoever loves his life loses it, and whoever hates his life in this world will keep it for eternal life" (John 12:24–25). Jesus was giving a key to fruitfulness in missions. When he tells us that we must hate our life it does not mean to have an unhealthy self-esteem. It has to do with forgetting our own desires. Missionaries must become absorbed in the life and culture of the community they are reaching; they must be planted in the soil. There are too many today who are unwilling to do this. They have one foot in and one foot out. My point is: count the cost of missions.

Also, remember that the goal of cross-cultural missions work, whether by African missionaries or Western missionaries, must be to make indigenous disciples. As fast as possible one should pass the work on to those from among the culture where they are working, so that they can run with the gospel in their own people group, and in neighboring peoples.

There are many wonderful missions organizations that you can work with if you feel called to missions. I would not recommend going it alone. Join with those who have experience and can equip and send you in the right way. We have a US missions program called *ACTS* which is training and sending laborers from America to the front lines. Please see the page at the back of this book for more information.

If you are interested in working with *Send56* there are several possibilities, both locally and internationally. We host groups and individuals for both short-term and long-term missions in Africa.

We also invite you to intern with us at our US office, based at the *International House of Prayer-Atlanta* in Georgia. You can be part of a 24/7 prayer environment as you help to bring awareness, prayer, and support to the missions movement in Africa! For more information about any of these possibilities, please contact us through our website www.Send56.org.

ACTS is a missions organization committed to equipping young leaders to pioneer the expansion of the gospel amongst unreached and unengaged people groups through worship, prayer and tireless church-planting.

Our ACTS School of Frontier Missions is a long-term training school designed to prepare young leaders to pioneer churches and houses of prayer in the Middle East, North Africa, Eurasia, Asia, and beyond. Students can be trained in either our Colorado Springs location or Atlanta location. Prospective students can apply today!

WWW.ANTIOCHCENTER.COM

(719) 785-8481

INFO@ANTIOCHCENTER.COM

Invite a Send56 Speaker

- Do you want to learn more about the unreached peoples group task?
- Do you have a heart to see Africa impacted with the gospel?
- Would your group or congregation like to be personally connected to the commission of our Lord Jesus?

Our US office in Atlanta is ready to serve you.
Simply reach us through the **www.Send56.org** contact form, or call 706-901-SEND(7363).
We look forward to meeting you!

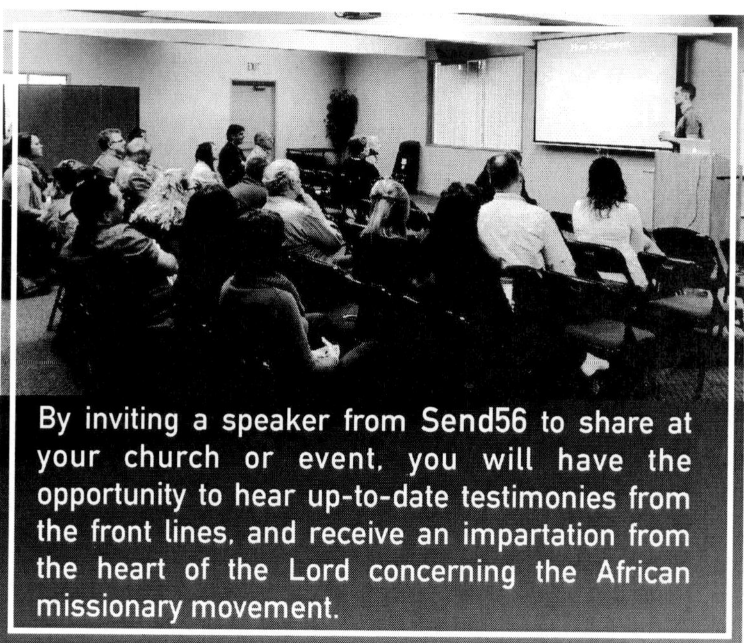

By inviting a speaker from Send56 to share at your church or event, you will have the opportunity to hear up-to-date testimonies from the front lines, and receive an impartation from the heart of the Lord concerning the African missionary movement.